GENDER IDENTITY

A Differentiation Model

ADVANCES IN PSYCHOANALYSIS: THEORY, RESEARCH, AND PRACTICE

A series of volumes edited by Joseph Reppen, Ph.D.

Advances in Psychoanalysis
Theory, Research, and Practice

Volume 2

GENDER IDENTITY

A Differentiation Model

Irene Fast
University of Michigan

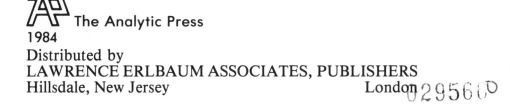 The Analytic Press

1984

Distributed by
LAWRENCE ERLBAUM ASSOCIATES, PUBLISHERS
Hillsdale, New Jersey   London

Lawrence Erlbaum Associates, Inc., Publishers
365 Broadway
Hillsdale, New Jersey 07642

Library of Congress Cataloging in Publication Data

Fast Irene.
  Gender identity.

  Bibliography: p.
  Includes index.
  1. Sex differences (Psychology) 2. Identity
(Psychology) I. Title.
BF692.2.F36 1984   155.3'3   84-6366
ISBN 0-88163-014-4
ISBN 0-88163-031-4 (ppk.)

Printed in the United States of America
10 9 8 7 6 5 4 3 2 1

Contents

Acknowledgments

It is a pleasure for me to express my appreciation to colleagues and friends generally, and in particular to Jonathan H. Slavin, Jeree Paul, and Peter Blos Jr., who, from the inception of the ideas presented in this book, have nurtured them, offered thoughtful suggestions, provided forums for their discussion, and encouraged me in their development. The notions elaborated here grew and were sharpened in the intellectual interplay of seminars and individual work with students. I am grateful for their continuing willingness to entertain ideas, to test them against their own observations, and to strike out in new directions of personal interest. Without their enthusiastic reception of the ideas and rigorous pursuit of their implications it is doubtful that this book would have been written.

For her generous editorial help and her able assistance in moving the book toward publication I thank Carole Berlin. The Horace H. Rackham School of Graduate Studies and the Department of Psychology of the University of Michigan offered financial assistance and I am grateful to them for it and for the support of the endeavor it implied.

Finally, I appreciate the permission from the editors of the *International Journal of Psycho-Analysis* and the *International Revue of Psycho-Analysis* to reprint the papers which, with minor alterations, comprise Chapters 1 and 2 of this volume.

GENDER IDENTITY

A Differentiation Model

Introduction

Psychoanalytic theories relevant to gender development remain centrally as Freud proposed them. From the beginning, questions have been raised about their implications for female development. Among major early critical evaluations are those by Horney (1926), Jones (1927), Rado (1933), and Jacobson, though Jacobson's valuable paper, first published in 1933, was not translated for English-speaking readers until much later (Jacobson, 1976). Attention continued to be drawn to observations in conflict with Freud's theory in subsequent publications, among them those by Zilboorg (1944), Greenacre (1950), Fraiberg (1972), and the collection of papers edited by Chasseguet-Smirgel (1970). Recently, in the context of intensified interest in the place of women in this society, as well as in more general changes in sexual mores and family patterns, controversial issues in Freud's theory have been raised with renewed vigor, marked by such collections of relevant papers as that edited by Blum (1977), and a recent issue of *The Psychoanalytic Revue* (Vol. 69, 1982) devoted entirely to the topic.

The areas of criticism go to the heart of Freud's theories. Biological evidence that the clitoris is not a male organ undermines the proposition that girls are anatomically bisexual at birth (the vagina a female organ, the clitoris a male one).

Observations, which are increasingly accepted, that girls are aware of their vaginas from an early age, challenge the notion of an early exclusively masculine orientation in girls centered in the (male) clitoris. General agreement that girls identify with the maternal qualities of their mothers makes unacceptable the formulation that girls' gender-relevant relations to their mothers are initially cross-sex ones based on their masculine orientations, and must be repudiated for normal development to occur. If these notions are accepted, every argument, biological and social, in support of Freud's proposition that the girl's development prior to her awareness of sex difference, is entirely male and masculine, is called into question. And if the girl's early development is not male and masculine, Freud's conception that her subsequent gender development occurs in reaction to an earlier masculinity, loses its power. Nevertheless, no comprehensive reformulation able to command general acceptance has emerged, and Freud's conceptualization of girls' gender development remains centrally influential in practice and in the clinical and theoretical literature, either directly or as the focus of disagreement.

No comparable questions have been raised about Freud's theories of male development. Nevertheless, growing bodies of literature suggest the need for revisions of these formulations as well. Stoller's (1968, 1975) seminal work suggests that social factors override physiological ones in human gender development, and that, in boys, strong early identifications with their mothers result in particular vulnerabilities in the establishment of a masculine gender identity. If that view gains acceptance, the proposition that boys' earliest sexual experiences are altogether male and masculine in anatomy, in associated sexual aims, and in cross-sex relations to their mothers, must be replaced. The growing body of literature that identifies an early feminine phase in boys, in which boys identify with their mothers in ways that include such female capacities as child-bearing, challenges both the notion of boys' exclusive masculinity and Freud's bisexuality theory, which posits a biologically based femininity in boys whose expression is in no way related to the mother, but occurs in wishes to be copulated with by the father and a willingness to bear a child for him. It will be argued here, moreover, that Freud's developmental theory and his theory of bisexuality in males are fundamentally incompatible in ways that urge the need for a revised formulation.

As Kuhn (1962) has persuasively argued, when, in any field, a growing consensus develops that an established theory can no longer accommodate accepted observations and perspectives, a multitude of theories and part-theories will be proposed. Out of these a new framework will gradually emerge, which achieves general acceptance. The time seems ripe for major developments in this direction in the area of gender development. The established body of critical evaluation and the current upsurge of interest in the topic is stimulating increased refinement of issues and proposed reformulations in many areas. It is the aim of this volume to offer one such reformulation, a relatively comprehensive one, in the hope that it can contribute to a gradually developing framework for understanding and exploring gender development, which will be widely acceptable to the relevant community of scholars and clinicians.

In forging a comprehensive model a number of parameters will be relevant. An acceptable framework must apply equally to gender development in males and in females. It must also account for typical differences observed in male and female development in this society, and, if possible, more generally. To be widely accepted, it must accommodate a broad range of established clinical observations, and show how their interpretations in the proposed model have greater usefulness than in the previously accepted one. Its usefulness will be enhanced, finally, to the degree that it can be shown to be capable of addressing conceptual problems unresolved in the previous framework, and to fruitfully articulate with other bodies of thought both within the parent theory (here, psychoanalytic psychology) and beyond it. The conceptualization proposed in these chapters addresses these issues in various ways. It does not aim for, and could not achieve, completeness. The aim, rather, is to address salient issues with sufficient thoroughness to permit a preliminary evaluation of the model's usefulness in application to issues of normal development and disturbance, in resolving recognized conceptual dilemmas, and in pointing the way for further exploration.

The model is one of psychological differentiation. It proposes that in early life children's gender-relevant experience is undifferentiated in a particular way. In both boys and girls development occurs in largely gender-appropriate directions due to social and biological influences, and is over-inclusive as a consequence of children's interactions with both male and female caregivers (usually the parents). However, children themselves do not categorize their experience in gender terms. It is in this respect that their experience is undifferentiated. The recognition of sex differences signals the beginning of gender differentiation: children's own categorization of their experience in gender terms. It is centrally a recognition of limits, that some sex and gender characteristics, uncritically assumed for themselves, belong exclusively to persons of the other sex, and is associated in both girls and boys with feelings of loss, denial, envy, and so forth. In subsequent differentiation processes (in psychoanalytic psychology, during the oedipal period), children elaborate their own sex-specific gender identities in identifications and same-sex relationships to one parent, and cross-sex relations to the other. In optimum outcome, children's narcissistic sense that all sex and gender possibilities are open to them is replaced by a sense of self as sex-specific in productive relation to other-sex persons recognized to be independent of self. These parameters of gender differentiation, which themselves apply to both girls and boys, pose different developmental problems for the two sexes and have differing modal outcomes, because in this society, the mother, herself female, is typically the major caregiver for both boys and girls.

The model is intended centrally to be a reformulation of Freud's gender-relevant theories as they refer to developments through the oedipal period, and their implications for later optimal and disturbed functioning. Therefore in this volume, major attention is devoted to the implications of the proposed view for different interpretations than Freud's, of the period before recognition of sex difference, of phenomena attendant on the recognition of the differences between the sexes, and of the subsequent (oedipal) period of gender identity consolidation. The model's application to clinical observation is examined in the context of major gender related disturbances (e.g., the perversions), and the re-interpretation of issues in well-known clinical cases (e.g., the patients familiarly known as Little Hans and the Wolf Man). More particularly the conceptual value of the model is explored for its usefulness in the resolution of conceptual problems (e.g., similarities and differences between girls and boys in their experience of sex difference related envies and castration anxieties; the relation of Freud's developmental and bisexuality theories in male development), and as it permits the integration of gender development formulations with other bodies of literature within psychoanalysis.

The model is explored, further, for possible integrations with psychology beyond psychoanalysis. In its structure as a model of psychological differentiation it promises to be congruent with the considerable body of theory whose focus is developmental differentiation, in which Werner's work (1961) and the work of Piaget are particularly well-known. The articulation of the proposed model of gender development with Piaget's model is elaborated, showing congruences between developments in identity out of egocentrism (Piaget) and out of narcissism (Freud), of which gender identity is a special case.

The individual chapters of this volume are intended to be self-contained pieces. They need not, therefore, be read consecutively. However, they do fall into a natural order, largely too, the order in which they were written. The first four follow a developmental sequence beginning with the period prior to the recognition of sex difference (Chapter 1), continuing with the phenomena attendant on the recognition of sex difference in girls (Chapter 2) and boys (Chapter 3), and culminating in the processes of gender differentiation specific to the oedipal period proper. Chapter 5 places the processes of gender identity development in the context of the general development of identity, as it represents transitions out of infantile narcissism (Freud) and primitive egocentrism (Piaget). Lastly, chapters 6 and 7 are in the nature of applications of the model, the first, an empirical test of some different implications of Freud's formulations and the proposed one, and the second, a clinical exploration of the case of the 'Wolf Man' in terms of themes implied by the proposed model.

REFERENCES

Blum, H. P. (Ed.) (1977). *Female Psychology.* New York: International Universities Press.

Chasseguet-Smirgel, J. (Ed.) (1970). *Female Sexuality.* Ann Arbor: University of Michigan Press.

Fraiberg, S. (1972). Some characteristics of genital arousal and discharge in latency girls. *Psychoanal. Study Child,* 27.

Greenacre, P. (1950). Special problems of early female sexual development. *Psychoanal. Study Child,* 5.

Horney, K. (1926). The flight from womanhood. *Internat. J. Psycho-Anal.,* 7: 324–339.

Jacobson, E. (1976). Ways of female superego formation and the female castration conflict. *Psychoanal. Q.,* 45: 525–538.

Jones, E. (1927). The early development of female sexuality. *Internat. J. Psycho-Anal.,* 8: 459–472.

Kuhn, T. S. (1962). *The Structure of Scientific Revolutions.* Chicago: University of Chicago Press.

Rado, W. (1933). Fear of castration in women. *Psychoanal. Q.,* 2: 425–475.

Stoller, R. J. (1968). *Sex and Gender.* New York: Aronson.

Stoller, R. J. (1975). *Sex and Gender.* Vol. 2, The Transexual Experiment. New York: Aronson.

Werner, H. (1961). *Comparative Psychology of Mental Development.* New York: Science Editions, Inc.

Zilboorg, C. (1944). Masculine and feminine: Some biological and cultural aspects. *Psychiatry,* 7: 257–296.

1 Developments in Gender Identity: The Original Matrix[1]

INTRODUCTION

In psychoanalytic theory the processes of the oedipal period are conceptualized as central in establishing gender identity. During this period the issues to be resolved and the problems in doing so are patterned in part by developments prior to that time, beginning with the original matrix out of which development proceeds.

As this matrix has been conceptualized in psychoanalytic theory, both boys and girls are originally male in functioning anatomical structure. The boy is unequivocally male in embryonic origins and anatomic structure. The girl is anatomically bisexual. The clitoris is embryologically male, the vagina female. Only the clitoris, anatomically a vestigial male organ, is of importance in the girl's early development.

Furthermore, the libidinal orientation in the early years of life has been conceptualized as masculine[2] in both sexes. The

---

[1]Previously published in the *Int. Rev. Psycho-Anal.*, (1978), 5, 265–273.

[2]I will follow Stoller (1968) in using the terms male and female when dealing with biological issues, masculine and feminine for matters of psychosocial origin. Some ambiguity occurs where origins are unclear or overlapping but in general the distinction is serviceable.

boy's development is therefore straightforwardly masculine. The girl's is more complicated. Through the phallic period the girl, in her sexual orientation and experience, is unequivocally masculine. Her genital interest and excitement are clitoral. The clitoris is, in her experience and in anatomical development, a small or vestigial penis. The quality of clitoral excitement, and its aims, are like those of the penis and thus, masculine. She normally has no knowledge of the vagina.

For both boys and girls the first emotional attachment is to the mother. For the boy this provides a heterosexual orientation in his earliest object relations. For the girl this first established relationship is a homosexual one.

The problems to be resolved in the oedipal period are determined in part by the characteristics of this original matrix. The boy has a secure masculine base in anatomy and instinctual orientation, and an orientation towards heterosexuality in his relationship to his mother. The oedipal processes begin for him when he perceives the father as rival for the mother. In order to resolve the oedipal dilemma, he gives up the (incestuous) relationship to the mother because of the threat of castration. He identifies with the father and accepts his values, thus taking a major step in establishing his masculine identity.

For the girl the problems of the oedipal period are different. The central issue for her is the achievement of a feminine gender identity and heterosexual orientation on a base that is male in its focus on the clitoris, masculine in instinctual orientation, and homosexual in primary object relationship. Oedipal processes begin for her when she becomes aware that her sexual organ is not as large as the boy's or is non-existent. In anger and disappointment she turns away from the mother. She turns to the father and substitutes a wish for a baby from him for the wish for a penis. In this way she takes a major step away from a homosexual orientation towards a heterosexual one. A further significant step in the establishment of her feminine identity remains to be taken after puberty when she transfers her interest from the clitoris with its male anatomy and masculine aims to the vagina with its feminine ones.

In barest outline these processes constitute the major developments in gender identity as Freud conceptualized them[3] and as they continue to be widely accepted in psychoanalytic thinking. As they concern the boy, they have provided a widely accepted formulation, elaborated in a multitude of directions. As they concern the girl, they have seemed less satisfactory. Freud himself offered the formulation in 1925 and reiterated it almost unchanged in 1931, but he continually repeated his dissatisfaction with it. Others, such as Horney (1926), Jacobson (1937), Thompson (1943), and Zilboorg (1944) have offered alternate approaches or modifications, but these have tended to remain unintegrated into the mainstream of psychoanalytic thought.

Recently, stimulated in part by renewed interest in the role of women in western society, but also by interest in more general changes in sexual mores and gender-relevant human characteristics, questions are being raised with renewed vigor about the psychoanalytic theory of gender identity development. New data and insights, experimentally and clinically based, add substance to issues being raised. Three are of particular interest here as immediately relevant to formulations about the original matrix.

The first concerns the biological origins of the clitoris. Basing his thinking on the known biology of his time, Freud conceptualized the clitoris as a vestigial male organ, and its libidinal orientation as masculine. Recent biological data,

---

[3]On almost every topic Freud expanded his views in various directions, altered them, and offered suggestive ideas which he did not integrate into the main line of his thinking. To assert, without complex qualifiers, that a particular formulation is Freud's, is therefore necessarily to do a disservice to the richness of his thinking. Nevertheless, it has seemed to me that a thorough re-examination of the psychoanalytic theory of gender development requires that its postulates be stated as explicitly as possible. Any reformulation must, of course, take into account the broadest possible range of data and insight, and the degree to which it can do so is a test of its usefulness. This chapter is limited to outlining one aspect of such reformulation and suggesting directions for its elaboration.

summarized by Stoller (1975), suggest that this conceptualization is not valid. The clitoris is not a vestigal male organ. It is female in anatomical origin, and the hypothesis that the instinctual aims associated with it are masculine is not supported by available biological data. If both clitoris and vagina are recognized to be female in origin, this anatomic base for the notion of greater bisexuality in women than in men is gone, and to whatever extent the psychological theory depends on this anatomic base, it is called into question. The notion that the girl is masculine in gender identity in the first years of life is not necessarily refuted, but it cannot be grounded on accepted data concerning biological origins. Finally, if the clitoris and vagina are both female in origin and integral parts of the female genital organization, the idea that the clitoris alone is functional in childhood without integration with or effect on the vagina is more difficult to accept and requires more support than when clitoris and vagina are seen as of distinctly different and sexually opposite anatomical origins.

A second body of data concerns the little girl's knowledge of her vagina in the early years of development. This issue is not new. Horney suggested as early as 1926 that young girls are aware of their vaginas. Freud, in 1931, and again in 1933, considered the fact that a number of clinicians had made similar observations, but he reasserted his earlier position (Freud, 1925) that the vagina was normally undiscovered by little girls. Jacobson, in 1936, emphasized the importance for optimal development of the girl's knowledge and exploration of her vagina, but this paper was not translated for English-speaking readers until the recent resurgence of interest in this topic. Recently, too, the contributions of Fraiberg (1972), Kestenberg (1968), Barnett (1966), and Torok (1970) address the question, and the notion that the girl has an early awareness of her vagina appears to be finding increasing acceptance in psychoanalytic thought.

Somewhat unexpectedly, the concept that the earliest matrix for gender identity development in boys is unequivocally male and masculine has also been called into question recently. The boy is at birth anatomically male, to whatever extent physiological factors are influential, the direction of his gender identity development is masculine. Stoller (1968) argues, however, that in humans physiological factors have an appreciable but secondary influence on gender identity, and that social factors generally override the physiological ones. Furthermore, he asserts that a major social factor for boys, as for girls, is the early identification with the mother. Thus, Freud emphasized the importance of male anatomy and instinctual orientation in contributing to boys' masculine identity; Stoller sees biological factors as relevant but of secondary importance. Freud focused on the boy's earliest relationship with the mother as heterosexual and contributing to his masculinity; Stoller and, in related work, Greenson (1968), emphasize the identificatory aspect of the boy's relation to the mother and therefore the uncertainty of his earliest sense of masculine identity. Therefore, while Freud considered the early gender development of the boy theoretically uninteresting because all major forces tend to strengthen his masculine orientation, Stoller suggests that contrary forces are normally operative, and that the boy cannot be thought of as unequivocally masculine in identity from the beginning.

These data and hypotheses suggest that neither girls nor boys are best conceptualized as male and masculine from the beginning. The problem, then, is to develop an alternate formulation: if boys and girls are not male and masculine in their earliest experience, what forms might their earliest gender experience take? If a male and masculine base does not underlie oedipal processes and to some extent pattern them, how might that base be conceptualized and what are the implications for understanding oedipal processes? Specifically, if the girl is no longer seen to be wholly male and masculine in orientation from the beginning, the central problem for her cannot be how a feminine identity can be built on a male and masculine base. If the boy is no longer seen to enter the oedipal period unequivocally male in anatomy, masculine in biologically based gender identity, and heterosexual in object relations, the influences on oedipal processes of his early development will need to be considered.

This chapter addresses only the first of these issues: the reconceptualization of the earliest base for the development of gender identity. The hypothesis to be proposed is that at birth boys are biologically male, girls female. Physiological factors probably contribute to sex difference in experience but are in the usual case overridden by social influences. From the time of sex ascription at birth, the caretaking environment treats girls and boys differently. Therefore boys' and girls' gender-related experience differs to some extent from the beginning, influenced by biological factors and differential handling by caretakers. With regard to gender awareness, it is proposed that girls' and boys' early experience is undifferentiated and overinclusive. That is, in the early processes of identification or establishment of self representations, the child has little sense that the characteristics of either femaleness or maleness, femininity or masculinity, are excluded for her or him respectively. Self representations or identifications are in this respect indiscriminate and overinclusive (though due to the caregiving practices of this society probably occur more extensively in relation to the mother than the father). At a later time, probably around the second half of the second year, the child can identify self and others as to maleness or femaleness. However, while such positive identification as 'girl' or 'boy' has been learned, *delimitation* of the characteristics of each has not. This delimitation occurs as part of the processes attendant on the child's recognition of sex difference. It involves renunciation of early gender-indiscriminate self representations and identifications now found to be physically impossible or gender-inappropriate (to grow a baby in one's body, to have a penis, to be physically active, to be tender, to be aggressive, and so forth). It requires attributing sex and gender characteristics, renounced for oneself, to members of the other sex. It includes recognition of the sex- and gender-related limits of the other sex.

This chapter offers evidence that an early period of development occurs in which boys' and girls' self representations or identifications include both male and female, masculine and feminine characteristics, and that there are subsequent processes of sex and gender differentiation and delimitation. Specifically, indications will be offered that early in development both boys and girls do assume that they have characteristics of both sexes. When they become aware of sex differences, probably in the third year of life, they feel a sense of loss or

deprivation, a requirement that they renounce self characteristics made their own through early identifications. Angry
and painful speculations occur about the reasons for such loss.
Even after the child has accepted the fact of his or her own
limits, a conviction may persist that it is a personal loss not
shared by others. The recognition of the sex- and gender-related limits of the other sex may be incompletely established.
Indications of residues of the early undifferentiated period
and of the subsequent processes of differentiation will be offered as they occur in the normal development of children, in
the arts and ceremonies of normal adulthood, and in cases of
emotional disturbance.

The proposed notion of an undifferentiated and overinclusive earliest matrix for gender identity development is in
some ways similar to Freud's formulation and in some ways
sharply different. Both frameworks posit an early developmental period before sex difference becomes salient and in
which children assume that all people are the same. It is in
the hypothesized character of that early sameness that the
proposed framework differs from the currently accepted one.
Freud's view was that boys and girls initially assume all people to be male and masculine. The proposed view is that initially boys and girls may internalize a wide range of characteristics of the people in their environment. No attribute is
excluded because it is inappropriate to the child's actual sex
and gender. Only retrospectively, when sex differences become salient, will the girl and the boy become aware that
attributes included in their developing self structures cannot
or must not in fact be theirs.

There is some evidence that children do have these overinclusive notions of their sex and gender possibilities. Girls'
notions that to be complete is to have a penis are well known.
The assumption is often made that such notions constitute a
wish to be a boy. There is, however, no explicit suggestion in
theory nor evidence in clinical experience that little girls
imagine that having a penis would mean *not* having the capacity to bear children.

More salient to the argument are boys' early ideas about
their sex and gender possibilities. The accepted view is that
boys are male and masculine from the beginning. If, as here

proposed, their experience is overinclusive rather than male and masculine, they, too, must have notions that all sexual possibilities are open to them: that, for instance, they too, can have male genitals and also have babies. Evidence is likely to be scanty because this notion has not been part of the theory directing observation. Nevertheless some evidence does exist. It is a familiar clinical observation that in boys, symptoms centering around defecation often represent various aspects of pregnancy fantasies. Erikson's (1950) case of Peter is a well-known example suggesting some directions such ideas may take. That is, some boys at least, conceive of themselves as able to grow children in their bodies.

More direct and explicit evidence comes from Freud's report of Little Hans' conversations with his father (Freud, 1909). In them, despite his father's demurrers Hans, at the age of five, continues to assert that boys can have babies, that his father can, and that he himself will. These notions in no evident way conflict with his sense of himself as a boy with a penis or with his masculine rivalry with his father.

Not only are there indications that girls and boys 'know' unreflectively that all sexual possibilities are open to them, but they attribute this same completeness to others. Freud recognized as early as 1908 that a pervasive fantasy of children is that mothers have penises, and he related the fantasy to the child's notion that everyone is the same. If one posits that in children's ideas everyone is the same, but sexually unlimited rather than male and masculine, one would expect that boys' notions that their mothers have penises would coexist with their knowledge that mothers have babies, and that if everyone is bisexually complete, fathers too have the capacity to bear children. In fact there is evidence that this is so. Clinical experience does not suggest that the notion of the mother having a penis means that the mother becomes 'boy,' or implies that she does not bear children. Little Hans, again, serves us well in his assertions that his father, like his mother can have babies, an assertion that in no way contravenes his sense of the father's dominating masculinity.

Clearly, this evidence for early notions of undifferentiated sexual completeness in boys and girls is not conclusive. The aim here can only be to indicate the kinds of implications that the proposed hypothesis would have and to show that some evidence for it is available.

The course of events when sex differences become salient will necessarily be different as envisioned in the two frameworks. The processes of differentiation from a prior undifferentiated state of male and masculine experience differ from those based on a prior bisexually overinclusive one. If the original matrix is male and masculine, only the girl need become aware of limits and deal with the consequences: she is in fact not complete as a male. The boy, accurately perceiving his male completeness, need make no such adjustment. However, if the earliest state is overinclusive in both boys and girls, then both must come to terms with limits.

The necessary coming to terms begins when children discover sex differences. Freud suggests that in part biological factors determine this awareness at about age two. Piaget (Flavell, 1963) suggests that the child attains cognitive capacities beginning at about that age that would make the necessary conceptualization possible. The triggering factor for the girl, in Freud's view, is her recognition that she is lacking a penis and that boys have one. With regard to boys, Freud made a suggestion that he did not pursue and that has found no secure place in psychoanalytic theory, but that seems illuminating for the hypotheses being proposed here. In 1908 he conjectured that the event triggering children's sexual interest was their curiosity about where babies come from. In 1925 Freud qualified this statement, saying that this may be the case for boys but it is definitely not so for girls: for girls sex differences become salient with their awareness that they lack the genital organ that boys have. These two notions taken together would suggest that the event precipitating interest in sex difference is the recognition of a limit: for boys the inability to grow babies, for girls the lack of a penis.

In the proposed framework, the notion that interest in sex difference is triggered by the recognition of something unexpectedly unavailable to oneself because of one's sex finds a ready place. Moreover, it seems likely that these triggers (female capacity to bear children, male possession of a penis) become foci or organizers for a larger array of attributes to be accepted for oneself or consigned to the other sex. As boys and girls become aware of sex difference, the gender-indiscriminate identifications or representations comprising their developing self structures must be tested against notions of their own sex and gender. Both girls and boys must begin to deal with necessary renunciations of those characteristics previously included among their self representations which cannot or must not be theirs. For the boy these might include not only biological matters such as the capacity to grow a baby in his body, but gender-related characteristics such as interpersonal interests expressed in doll-play, delight in color, music or art, and free emotional expression. For the girl the focal issue is likely to be that she does not have a penis, but that may become for her the organizer and symbol of such other renunciations as intellectual precocity, physical vigor, freedom of aggressive expression.

The significance of this recognition for the girl has been emphasized in psychoanalytic literature. The importance of the complementary event for boys has not gone unnoticed but has as yet had no comparably intensive investigation. Nevertheless, Freud suggested far-reaching effects of the boy's recognition of the mother's central role in the origin of babies and his concern about a role for males, 'This brooding and doubting [about the father's role], however, becomes the prototype of all later intellectual work directed towards the solution of problems and the first failure has a crippling effect on the child's future' (1908, p. 219).

The differentiation processes and phenomena observed to occur in the girl as she makes her peace with the facts of sex difference include feelings that the absence of the penis is a loss, demands for restitution of it, convictions that the mother can make good the loss, painful speculations about the loss as punishment, beliefs (long after she has given up the idea of having a penis herself) that other women are not as ill-equipped as she is, and assumptions that boys suffer no lack. Similar processes in boys and the ways they come to terms with their recognition of limits have not been extensively observed, though some clinical observations noted below offer retrospective data.

If the notion of an undifferentiated and over-inclusive original matrix for gender development and something like the hypothesized differentiation processes occur when sex differences become salient in the course of development, then it should be possible to find residues of such early events in the processes of normal living and, perhaps more vividly, in cases of disturbed development. To the extent that art and mythology express ideas prevalent in a culture, the occurrence of bisexual figures in primitive art may suggest residues of ideas normal in early childhood. The myth of Hermaphroditus, in whom a man and a woman were united, suggests again that the notion of bisexual completeness is not altogether foreign, and myths in which males bear children, as Zeus bears Althena, suggest a possible prevalence in men of fantasies that they, too, can give birth.

Kubie (1974) and Bettelheim (1954) have drawn attention to wishes in men and in women to have the attributes of the other sex in addition to their own, and have shown relationships between the occurrence of such wishes in cases of disturbance and in the normal cultural experience. Kubie titles his paper 'The Drive to Become Both Sexes.' He argues that in every person there is such a drive and that 'the unconscious drive is *not* to give up the gender to which one was born but to supplement or complement it by developing side by side with it the opposite gender, thereby ending up as both.' He first indicates the prevalence of such themes in art and literature. Then, with extensive clinical material he traces effects of such wishes in such varied domains as disturbances in capacities for work, in processes of courtship, in marriage choices, in psychotic disorganization, in particular difficulties in the end-phases of treatment. Bettelheim (1954) focuses on the theme of the duality of the sexes as he was able to observe it in children and as he hypothesizes it to be central in the initiation rites of primitive cultures. He argues that 'one sex feels envy in regard to the sexual organs and functions of the other,' and that all people wish to have the genitalia of the other sex in addition to their own. He gives examples from his experience with children, of boys' obsessional wishes to possess both male and female genitalia and of corresponding wishes in girls. In his focus on initiation rites he suggests that these ceremonies, involving complex ways of taking the roles and functions of one's own and of the opposite sex, are methods of coming to terms with the duality of the sexes, of giving up notions that one can be bisexually complete, and of finally committing oneself to one's appropriate sex role. Neither Kubie nor Bettelheim suggest an original matrix such as the one proposed here, but their findings are clearly congruent with such a hypothesis rather than with one in which boys and girls are male and masculine in their early experience.

Personal observations of relevant clinical material are beginning to accrue, though confidentiality issues prohibit extended case elaboration at this time. They suggest that residues of primitive notions of bisexual wholeness and of the processes of sexual and gender differentiation proposed here may present themselves in clinical work in the complicated ways typical of any aspect of development. For a young man unusually persistent ideas of bisexual wholeness underlay fears of homosexuality and were related to a long-standing sense that he lived both for himself and for a dead sister. In the therapy of a woman they were linked to problems of self–other differentiation. One expression of them was a notion that became conscious in the course of treatment, that in her marriage her husband was not an autonomous individual, but rather served to give her the attributes she required to be complete. To be pregnant as well was the apogee: it implied having the unmistakable insignia of both maleness and femaleness. When the processes of working through these issues were most intense, she suffered transitory but frightening episodes in which she experienced herself as physically merged with him, unable to sense whether a body part was in fact hers or his. Forms that notions of incompleteness consequent to the recognition of limits may take in women are clinically familiar, but have been less extensively explored in men. In one man a sudden acute awareness of his sexual partner's lack of a penis subsumed not only castration fears but also a sense of his own limits: his lack of ability to bear children, a theme that subsequently led to explorations of work difficulties focusing on a sensed inability to be creative or to produce anything worthwhile. In another, one theme in his castration anxiety reflected a repudiated wish: the yearning to recapture the possibility of interpersonal intimacy by giving up the phallic insignia of masculinity that meant an extreme of objectivity and impersonality to him. Persisting notions that others do not suffer the same limits as oneself also occur in both men and women about members of their own and the opposite sex. For one young women they underlay an intensely critical attitude towards other women's appearance, expressed as: 'What's she got that I haven't got?' In a sexually inhibited man they underlay his sense that he had no way to understand women. Women could understand one another because they had the same experience. Other men, too, could understand women. Behind his notion that these men were 'experienced' as he was not, lay a profound sense that his sex and gender limits were losses not shared by other men or by women.

These examples, derived from observations of normal development, representations in cultural artifacts and ceremonies, and evidence from clinical work, have been presented in support of a proposed reconceptualization of the original matrix from which gender identity develops. The major difference between this framework and the one Freud proposed is that in Freud's view both boys and girls are originally masculine in their experience, whereas in the one proposed, they are overinclusive in their early experience, not aware of limitations inherent in being of a particular sex. Other differences in conceptualization follow from this one. Freud noted that children have ideas that their mothers have penises. The proposed framework suggests that initially children have ideas of mothers with penises and fathers able to have babies, and that even when they have given up notions of such bisexual completeness in themselves they may still attribute it to others. In Freud's view, when sex difference becomes salient for children only the girl must come to terms with limits: she becomes aware that she has no penis. In the proposed view both boys and girls must become aware of them: the girl must give up the possibility of having a penis and gender-inappropriate self representations; the boy becomes aware that only mothers bear babies and must renounce self aspects previously internalized but now found to be inappropriate to his gender. In Freud's view, because only the girl is lacking, only the girl is envious of the other sex. In the proposed one, the boy's envy finds a place as well. In Freud's view the girl becomes aware that she has no penis in the context of her early masculinity. In the proposed view, both girl and boy become aware they do not have the attributes of the other sex in the context of experience that also includes awareness of their own actual sexual and gender attributes. In the accepted model the female capacity to bear children plays little part. In the proposed framework it is the trigger for the boy's interest in sex difference.

Because the oedipal period has been viewed as central for the establishment of gender identity, these formulations must be seen in terms of their implications for the conceptualization of oedipal processes as well. Detailed elaboration is reserved for a later chapter, but indications can be given here of directions of investigation. For the most part they imply expansion of areas of inquiry rather than denying the importance of those heretofore considered central. A central underlying focus is the place of the mother and of the child's feminine characteristics in the oedipal triangle. In current theory the boy is seen to enter the oedipal period masculine in gender identity and heterosexual in object orientation. His entry into the oedipal period is signalled by rivalry with his father for his mother. Major accomplishments of that period are the establishment of an identification with the father and his values, and under threat of castration, giving up his incestuous relationships to his mother.

In the proposed framework, he is seen to enter the oedipal period, not unequivocally masculine but overinclusive in his experience. Entry into the oedipal period requires recognition of sex difference. Therefore it is seen to be signalled by both the boy's rivalry with the father *and* his recognition of the

requirement that he relinquish claim to attributes appropriate only to girls and women. His relationship to the mother
has been objectively heterosexual since birth, but is hypothesized here to be largely gender-undifferentiated in his experience. Now it becomes masculine in relation to his mother as
specifically feminine. One important theme in the boy's relationship to the father is the achievement of a specifically masculine identification. It involves both giving up claim to
female/feminine attributes and also sufficiently resolving the
attendant envy, sense of loss, and so on, to commit himself to
the elaboration of his masculinity. Castration anxiety in this
context is seen to derive its power not only from the rivalry-
based threat from the father but *also* from the boy's repudiated wishes for the characteristics of the other sex. Masculine
protest, the contempt for all things feminine, is seen to be,
like its counterpart, women's contempt for all things masculine, a defensive aversion to desired characteristics.

The central problem of the oedipal period for the girl, as
Freud saw it, is the construction of a feminine identity on the
masculine base with which she enters the oedipal period. Her
entry into the oedipal period is triggered by her recognition
that she has no penis. In anger and disappointment she turns
from her mother to her father and substitutes a wish for a
baby for the wish for a penis.

In the proposed framework she is seen to enter the oedipal
period with female genitals rather than ones that are partly
male and partly unknown. Her gender experience is overinclusive rather than altogether masculine. The recognition
that she has no penis confronts her with limits rather than
the loss of the only known genital. It occurs in the context of
self representations of her female body and feminine gender
characteristics. Her envy of the penis is not bedrock, responsive to actual biological superiority of the male. It is responsive to a forced recognition of limits and is resolved in a
change of focus from this lack, to focus on female and feminine
characteristics objectively and experientially present. The relationship to the mother is not only one of hatred and disappointment but also one of specifically feminine identification

and relationship. The wish for a baby from the father is not only a turning away from the mother, but also an identification with her in her specifically female child-bearing capacity.

SUMMARY

Recent clinical and experimental observations as well as vigorous social pressure have encouraged re-examination of the psychoanalytic conceptualization of the development of gender identity. In the theory the processes in the oedipal period are seen to be central in the establishment of gender identity. These processes are patterned in part by prior developments beginning in the original matrix, the base from which development proceeds. This chapter has focused on this hypothesized earliest experience.

The original matrix as proposed by Freud posits that boys and girls are male in functioning anatomy and masculine in gender orientation in the first years of life. Based on their earliest relationship to the mother, boys are heterosexual and girls homosexual in object orientation. A revision of this conceptualization is proposed and its implications for oedipal processes summarized. Rather than male and masculine in earliest gender orientation, children are hypothesized to be overinclusive in their experience, not attuned to sex difference or aware of the limitations inherent in belonging to a particular sex. Interest in sex difference begins with the recognition of limits: the boy's interest in the mother's place in the origin of babies, the girl's recognition that she has no penis.

Both boys and girls must come to terms with their limits. In the course of doing so both may envy the sex and gender attributes of the other sex. Both may perceive the fact of not having those attributes as a loss or an incompleteness, and demand restitution. Both may, after they have recognized their own limits, attribute bisexual 'completeness' to others. For both, success in coming to terms with limits requires giving up a focus on not having the sexual attributes of the other sex and committing oneself to one's own actual sexual identity. Evidence from normal development, cultural artifacts, and ceremonies, and psychopathology is brought to bear in support of these hypotheses.

REFERENCES

Barnett, M. C. (1966). Vaginal awareness in the infancy and childhood of girls. *J. Am. psychoanal. Ass.* **14,** 129–141.

Bettelheim, B. (1954). *Symbolic Wounds.* Glencoe, Ill.: Free Press.

Erikson, E. H. (1950). *Childhood and Society.* New York: Norton.

Flavell, J. H. (1963). *The Developmental Psychology of Jean Piaget.* London: Van Nostrand.

Fraiberg, S. (1972). Some characteristics of genital arousal and discharge in latency girls. *Psychoanal. Study Child,* **27.**

Freud, S. (1908). On the sexual theories of children. *S.E.* **9.**

Freud, S. (1909). Analysis of a phobia in a five-year-old boy. *S.E.* **10.**

Freud, S. (1925). Some physical consequences of the anatomical distinction between the sexes. *S.E.* **19.**

Freud, S. (1931). Female sexuality. *S.E.* **21.**

Freud, S. (1933). New introductory lectures on psychoanalysis: xxxiii. *S.E.* **22.**

Greenson, R. R. (1968). Dis-identifying from the mother: its special importance for the boy. *Int. J. Psycho-Anal.* **49,** 370–374.

Horney, K. (1926). The flight from womanhood. *Int. J. Psycho-Anal.* **7,** 324–339.

Jacobson, E. (1936). On the development of the girl's wish for a child. *Psychoanal. Q.* **37,** (1968), 523–538.

Jacobson, E. (1937). Ways of female superego formation and the female castration conflict. *Psychoanal. Q.* **45,** (1976), 525–535.

Kestenberg, J. S. (1968). Outside and inside, male and female. *J. Am. psychoanal. Ass.* **16,** 457–520.

Kubie, L. S. (1974). The drive to become both sexes. *Psychoanal. Q.* **43,** 349–426.

Stoller, R. J. (1968). *Sex and Gender,* vol. 1. New York: Aronson.

Stoller, R. J. (1975). *Sex and Gender,* vol. 2: *The Transsexual Experiment.* New York: Aronson.

Thompson, C. (1943). 'Penis envy' in women. *Psychiatry* **6,** 123–125.

Torok, M. (1970). The significance of penis envy in women. In J. Chasseguet-Smirgel (ed.), *Female Sexuality.* Ann Arbor: Univ. of Michigan Press.

Zilboorg, C. (1944). Masculine and feminine: some biological and cultural aspects. *Psychiatry* **7,** 257–296.

2 Gender Differentiation in Girls[1]

INTRODUCTION

Freud's theory of female sexuality has never been entirely satisfactory. Nevertheless, it has been hard to give up. A major reason has been that a number of its major tenets have been regularly validated in clinical observation. A major developmental advance towards femininity appears to occur in about the third year of life. This advance is triggered by the girl's becoming focally aware of sex difference. Her reaction to that recognition tends to be expressed as a sense of loss or injury as if she had had male genitalia and lost them, and to be accompanied by envy and demands for restitution. Subsequent changes occur in her relations to her mother and father. A wish for a baby supplants an earlier wish/demand for maleness.

Freud's theory integrating these materials postulates that they represent the process of change in the girl's sex and gender orientation from male to female. Prior to becoming aware of sex difference, he suggests, the girl is in every relevant respect masculine in sexual orientation. Her develop-

---

[1]Previously published, with minor differences, *Int. J. Psycho-Anal.* (1979)*60,* 443–453.

mental task, when sex difference becomes focal, is to establish a feminine gender identity on this masculine base. The weight of current evidence suggests that this formulation is no longer tenable.

This chapter proposes an alternate framework. It suggests that the observed developments in gender identity following recognition of sex difference can be understood as differentiation phenomena. Prior to awareness of sex difference, major developments in that direction have occurred but have not yet been categorized specifically in gender terms. When the girl becomes aware of sex difference she develops a complex sense of femininity and herself as feminine in relation to a concurrently developing sense of masculinity attributed to males and experienced in relation to them. Comparable processes occur in boys but elaboration of them is reserved for a later discussion. These developments can be understood as reflections of this differentiation process.

FREUD'S CONCEPTUALIZATION OF FEMININE DEVELOPMENT

In Freud's view the girl's gender-related development prior to her awareness of sex difference is in all respects male and masculine. The genital anatomy of the girl is bisexual. Only the vagina is female; the clitoris is male in embryological origin and masculine in associated libidinal orientation. Normally the vagina is unknown to the girl before puberty; only the clitoris is a part of her experience. When, in the course of development, instinctual interest shifts from the oral and anal zones to the genital one the girl's pleasurable excitements are exactly like the boy's. They are focused on the clitoris and the related interests are masculine. The girl's first attachment, to her mother, predisposes her to homosexual rather than heterosexual relationships. Thus, at this point in development, in the anatomy available to her experience, in the related genital aims, and in interpersonal predisposition 'the little girl is in all respects a little man,' (Freud, 1933).

It is on this male and masculine base that femininity must develop. The process centrally involves overcoming this biologically and socially based masculinity. It begins when the girl becomes focally aware of sex difference. The difference that she experiences is that her genital organ is inferior to the boy's. This inferiority has particular salience because the girl becomes aware of it at a time when the clitoris has become a major source of satisfaction and is central in the organization of her experience (as oral and anal zones had been previously). Now she must renounce this genitality because it is male. She has no experiential knowledge of a genital organ that is female and can provide the center for feminine gender identity.

Her reaction is profound. She feels herself to have sustained a major loss. This loss is represented in her experience as a castration. She feels an intense envy of the boy. Developments in response to this castration experience begin the process of substituting a feminine for a masculine gender identity. The girl, in disappointment and dissatisfaction with her genital organ gives up clitoral masturbation, thus turning away from that focus for the elaboration of her masculinity. In her behavior she turns from an active to a passive and masochistic orientation, thus from a masculine to a feminine one. She turns away from the mother in disappointment at and blame for her genital inferiority, thus diminishing the impetus towards a homosexual orientation. She turns towards the father, beginning the establishment of heterosexuality. She substitutes a wish for a child from him for the wish for a penis, thus strengthening the heterosexual bond and providing a way to overcome her penis envy.

This theory has remained dominant in psychoanalytic psychology. It has not been discarded and in practice and clinical literature is not ignored. However, major propositions of the theory have been examined and found to be untenable. Current biological evidence indicates that the clitoris cannot be considered an anatomically male organ. To the extent that instinctual aims are physiological and influence gender behavior the evidence suggests that they do it in a gender appropriate direction (Stoller, 1968). The weight of clinical evidence is increasingly against the notion that the girl is aware only of her clitoris in early life (Greenacre, 1950; Kestenberg, 1968; Torok, 1970; Fraiberg, 1972) and observational data offer no support for it (Galenson & Roiphe, 1977; Kleeman, 1977; Parens, Pollack, Stern, & Kramer, 1977). The notion that the girl's relationship to her mother predisposes her to a masculine orientation and to homosexuality is no longer widely accepted.

These objections to Freud's formulation are increasingly accepted as valid and the relevant propositions no longer asserted. However, the implications for his theory of the development of femininity have not been examined and accepted. If the clitoris is not anatomically male, if gender-relevant physiological factors do not dispose the girl to masculinity, if the girl's genital experience includes the vagina as well as the clitoris, and if the mother-child relationship disposes her to femininity, then every argument, biological and social, that Freud offers in support of his notion that the girl's development prior to her awareness of sex difference is male and masculine, is called into question. His conceptualization of developments subsequent to the beginning awareness of sex difference is then also undermined. If the girl's development to that time is not male and masculine, the subsequent development of femininity cannot be reactive to her earlier maleness.

The gender differentiation theory is an attempt to provide an alternative framework to conceptualize those developments.

AN ALTERNATE CONCEPTUALIZATION: GENDER DIFFERENTIATION

In psychoanalytic psychology notions of differentiation have been fruitful in exploring a number of areas of development. Among these are the child's categorizations of reality experience into the subjective and the objective, primitive self-other unity into self and other distinct from one another, the illusion of omnipotence into appreciation of personal intention and impersonal causality.

These differentiation processes have similar parameters. In each case developments in differentiation proceed from a prior undifferentiated state. The subjective experience of that state is a narcissistic one of unlimited possibility: before reality testing subjective experience is not differentiated; before learning appropriately to attribute cause the child has an inchoate sense that his wants are the arbiters of events; and before self-other differentiation characteristics appropriately attributed to self and to the other occur within the primitive self boundary.

The process of differentiation involves a recategorization of experience. Each differentiated pattern is elaborated and articulated in distinctive ways (e.g. subjective reality experience, distinct from the objective, is refined into memory, anticipation, fantasy, and the intricacies of drama, lying, speculation, illusion and so forth). Both differentiated patterns have valid places in experience (subjective reality experience is not rejected as unreal in favor of the objective; personal intention is neither held to be of paramount importance nor denied as ephemeral). One differentiation product is elaborated as part of self, the other defined as independent of self (subjective reality, intention, and self as distinct from objective reality, impersonal causality, other person). In each case relationship between the two differentiation products, one an aspect of self, the other independent of self, replaces elaboration of both within the self. In other words, object relation replaces narcissistic elaboration.

In the process of differentiation typical difficulties tend to occur. The transition out of the undifferentiated experience of unlimited possibility may be experienced as involving an actual loss or deprivation (observable clinically in yearning for what is felt to be an actual lost omnipotence, feelings that with reality testing an existing power to create reality is taken away, feelings of actual deprivation at evidence of the other's independence of oneself). The loss may be experienced as total (if not omnipotence then powerlessness, if not unity with the other then utterly without connection, if not creator of reality then altogether without influence). It may be felt as a personal loss not shared by others. Angry and painful rumination may occur about the reason for the deprivation. A major struggle in the process of differentiation is to overcome the tendency towards return to earlier narcissistic notions (the inappropriate inclusion in the self of what must be recognized as independent of self, the attribution of narcissistic completeness to the other and nothingness to the self, the regressive replacement of relationship by assertion of narcissistic control).

Normally, such difficulties are transient. They are replaced by a renewed sense of personal centrality, not now the original one of unlimited potential but a delimited and more complexly articulated one experienced to be in productive relationship to that which is independent of self. When the differentiation processes have not been altogether successful, unresolved issues may become foci of disturbance.

These parameters of differentiation processes can be applied to developments in gender identity in both boys and girls. An early undifferentiated stage is postulated in which the child's sense of sex and gender potential is not limited by its actual sex. This is different from Freud's notion of girls' and boys' early masculinity. The characteristics of that early undifferentiated period have been elaborated in Chapter 1, but will be summarized below as they pertain to the girl's development.

The outcome, when differentiation has been successfully completed, is also different than that anticipated by Freud. He suggests that it is characteristic of women to be passive and masochistic. Their female genital sexuality does not emerge until adolescence or adulthood, is dependent on the man for its awakening, is passive in nature, and is weaker than the man's in both direct and sublimated expression. The woman's state is factually a castrated one; she repudiates it as inferior as indeed it is; her biologically based envy is inherent in the feminine condition.

From a gender differentiation perspective, the normal outcome is postulated to be analogous to that of other differentiations. The girl has a renewed sense of personal centrality. It is not now the narcissistic one of unlimited potential. It is a delimited one of herself as specifically feminine identified with and related to females as specifically feminine and in productive relationship to males now perceived in masculine terms and as independent of herself.

The processes of gender differentiation are hypothesized to have the same parameters as the other differentiations. The observational phenomena of feminine development beginning with the recognition of sex difference are those familiar to psychoanalysis. They begin with the girl's recognition of sex difference. The sharp sense of loss that accompanies this awareness is seen in differentiation terms to be responsive to her recognition that she is not unlimited, that those things tied to sex and gender and unequivocally male are to be lost to her. The penis as focus for her sense of loss and her demand for restitution is not a wish to be male but a wish for unlimited possibility. Her feeling that she has sustained an actual genital loss is similar to feelings attendant on giving up the illusion of omnipotence or self-other unity. Her feeling that the male has everything and she nothing is a misconception that alternates (or co-exists) with her sense that she has everything, he nothing.

The differentiation processes that ensue involve a re-categorization of her experience in gender terms. Notions of masculinity as well as femininity become complexly articulated. Both have validity, one (femininity) within the self, the other (masculinity) independent of self and in reciprocal relation to it. Female genitality is integrated into the girl's body image and gender identity; male genitality, reciprocal to it, is attributed to boys. The developing conceptualizations of femininity and masculinity are expressed and refined in relation to the mother and father now newly appreciated in gender terms. One importance of the wish for a baby may be that it simultaneously expresses the same-sex identification with the mother and the cross-sex relation to the father.

Difficulties in the girl's development of feminine gender identity are seen to reflect problems in differentiation. In

Freud's view the girl's central struggle is to overcome her masculinity; in the differentiation framework it is to overcome her narcissism.

TOWARDS THE RECOGNITION OF SEX DIFFERENCE

The hypothesized undifferentiated state prior to the girl's recognition of sex difference is both similar to and different from the undifferentiated state as Freud describes it. Both conceptualizations postulate that prior to this period the girl does not conceptualize her experience in gender terms. Unlike the proposed view, however, Freud suggests that the gender-relevant prior development of the girl predisposes her to a male and masculine orientation.

The differentiation paradigm suggests that the girl's genital organization is female. Experiences localized in genitals contribute to her body image from birth. Masturbatory focus on that area appears to begin in the second year of life. Physiological contributions to gender-specific behavior, to the extent that they occur, predispose the girl in the direction of her actual sex. Social influences on gender development begin with sex ascription at birth. From that time the caregiving environment treats girls and boys differently. The mother (or substitute caregiver) is the predominant person in the girl's life, but by the end of the first year the girl has established differential relationships to father and to mother. By about two years of age she is able to attribute masculinity or femininity to her self and others.

Though these developmental foundations for gender identity have occurred prior to the girl's focal awareness of sex difference, it is only in the context of that awareness that the recategorization of her experience in gender terms takes place. Before that time, as data from observations of early development, clinical explorations with disturbed children and adults, and cultural myth and ceremony suggest, there is a regularly occurring developmental period in which sex and gender characteristics are indiscriminately assumed for oneself without limitations based on one's actual sex.

It is on the base of such undifferentiated notions of sex and gender that the girl becomes focally aware of sex difference. Rather than male and masculine in her prior experience she is hypothesized to have made major developments in the feminine direction. Rather than an undifferentiated sense of herself whose components are masculine she is hypothesized to have an undifferentiated and unlimited sense of her sex and gender potential.

One regularly observed reaction of the little girl to becoming aware of sex difference is a sense of loss or of damage. In recent observational studies (Parens et al., 1977; Galenson & Roiphe, 1977) it appears to be expressed in sudden and intense concerns about things that are broken. A hole in a sock, a broken cracker, a cracked lollipop evoke major protest and demand for repair. Galenson and Roiphe relate the loss specifically to the absence of a penis and the girl's wish for one, expressed in girls' collecting their fathers' pens, mislabeling dolls, and pictures as boys, asking their mothers where their own or their mother's penis is. The concern is serious enough, Galenson and Roiphe believe, to result in temporary affective changes such as unusual quietness, loss of zest, or appearance of sadness. In cases of disturbed development, particularly after traumatic separations, Galenson and Roiphe note more marked reactions. Where early development has not been disturbed, however, these reactions are of only moderate intensity and are transient.

Abraham (1920) and Rado (1933) offer descriptions of this reaction as they observed it in clinical work with adults. They suggest that it is represented in women's anxieties related to dental procedures, to manicures, or in particular reactions to blood, the sight of injuries, and so on. Abraham relates the sense of loss or injury specifically to women's felt lack of a penis. He gives numerous examples of female patients' wishes to have one. One patient dreamt 'I am the fortunate possessor of a penis.' Another liked to hold her finger in such a way that the shadow of her naked body would seem to show a penis. A third wished to be a female Napoleon. A fourth had a dream of a pocket with a syringe in which the syringe represented a penis.

The validity of the clinical observation of womens' sense that they lack, and want, male genitalia has generally not been challenged in the relevant literature, and it is the *interpretation* of those observations that is in question here. In Freud's view the girl's interest in sex difference is signalled by her focal awareness of the penis. She sees that the boy has a penis and she does not. Her feeling is of being *castrated*. Later clinically-observed feelings of the loss or lack of a penis reflect this feeling of *castration*.

In the differentiation framework the girl's sense of loss, when she becomes aware that the boy has a penis and she does not, is interpreted differently. It is viewed as representing the girl's recognition that not all sex and gender possibilities are open to her. She perceives this as a loss and protests against it. Later clinically observed feelings of wanting or lacking a penis, similarly reflect a demand for a lost experience of unlimited potential, a state of narcissistic completeness.

The term castration, referring to the girl's sense of loss or injury when the awareness of sex difference becomes focal, is an ambiguous one in psychoanalytic usage. One dimension of it in Freud's framework is that it represents the loss of the only known genital organ and, implicitly, the instinctual experience that accompanies it. That is, the only genital experience known to boys and girls in childhood is male. Not to have a male genital organ is to have none, to be in this sense castrated.

The clinical problem, when women give indication of feelings that they lack a penis and want one, is that they have failed to give up their masculinity. The clinical aim is to induce them to give it up, to recognize and accept their castrated state. Freud (1937) expresses his pessimism about achieving this. He suggests that male genitality is objectively superior, that repudiation of femininity by both men and women is 'a biological fact' and that it may not be possible satisfactorily to complete the analysis of women in this respect.

The differentiation framework suggests an alternate perspective: the woman's feelings that she has lost male genitalia, that therefore all is lost, feelings of repudiating femininity and of wanting a male genital organ are seen to be residues of an early stage in the differentiation process. They represent her awareness that she is not limitless in sex and gender potential and her protest against that fact.

The characteristics of penis envy itself support this interpretation. The maleness that is envied is not maleness as it objectively exists. It is envy of a 'maleness' that would give one infinite power for good or evil, total security, absolute freedom, immunity from anxiety or guilt and the fulfilment of all wishes. That is, the girl's demand for a penis is a demand, now in the context of gender differentiation, for limitlessness, which has the characteristics of developmentally early narcissistic experience, not for a realistic, differentiated maleness.

Developmental and clinical observations of the girl's or woman's feeling that she lacks, and wants, a penis are congruent with this interpretation as well, though the interpretation given has been different. Abraham interprets womens' wishes, illusions, dreams, and ambitions to have a penis as wishes to be male, but in no example does this wish involve a repudiation of actual femininity, and in some, like the dream of the syringe in the pocket or the wish to be a female Napoleon, the wish not to give up either male or female characteristics seems clear. Deutsch (1933), similarly, interprets as castration anxiety and the wish to be a man, the girl's wish to have babies by immaculate conception or parthenogenesis. It reflects her fantasy, Deutsch suggests, that she can have a baby without a man, that anything a man can do she can also do. But to have a baby without a father seems to assert the possession of both maleness and femaleness, rather than just a wish to be a man. Developmental observations in settings with extensive opportunity for observation (Parens *et al.*, 1977; Galenson & Roiphe, 1977) or more casually made observations are also congruent with the differentiation hypothesis. A little girl Abraham (1920) describes, who in her ceremonious gift of a cigar to her mother seems to act out her wish that mothers should have penises, seems not to wish her mother to stop being a mother, but to have maleness *as well*. The young woman in Freud's example (1923) who remembered thinking as a young girl that her mother and her mother's friends had penises showed no sign of thinking, or wishing that they were men. The readily observed idea in children that their mothers have penises in no way detracts from their recognition of their mother's femininity. That is, the sensed loss of maleness seems to represent to the girl (woman) the loss of unlimited potential. To have maleness (or male genitalia) would make her complete. Her wish is not to be male instead of female, but to be unlimited instead of female. The clinical problem, then, is not to induce the woman to accept the fact of her inferiority to males, or castrated state. It is to help her give up the illusion of unlimited potential.

A second dimension of the meaning of the term castration in relation to the girl's sense of loss when she becomes aware of sex difference involves Freud's conception that the girl's early genital experience is focused exclusively on the clitoris. Because such experience is masculine in character, continued involvement in clitoral masturbation predisposes the girl toward excessive masculinity, and in normal development it terminates when the girl becomes aware of sex difference. There is no alternative feminine genital sexuality available to her in childhood. In this sense, as well, her castration is actual: the girl renounces all experience of genital satisfaction.

The proposed framework postulates that anatomically the girl's genital organization is female, and that to the extent that physiological forces influence her gender behavior they do so in a feminine direction. Prior to her becoming focally aware of sex difference she does not categorize her genital experience as male or female. The normal outcome of the differentiation process is that the girl categorizes her genital experience as feminine. Her genital sexuality is integrated into her body image as 'girl' and into her feminine gender identity. That is, her *objectively* female genitalia are now experienced *subjectively* as female.

This formulation reopens a number of issues. One concerns the availability of the girl's genitalia to her experience. Freud's view was that she was normally aware only of her clitoris. Clinical observation (Greenacre, 1950; Kestenberg,

1968; Fraiberg, 1972) and direct observation of children (Galenson & Roiphe, 1977; Parens *et al.*, 1977) suggest the possibility that her genitalia as a whole may be part of her experience.

A second issue concerns the girl's dichotomization of her genital experience as partly male and partly female. Freud's view is that this is biologically based and inevitable. The proposed framework opens the issue for exploration. If the girl's genitalia are objectively female it becomes reasonable to explore the circumstances in which she might experience them as partly male and partly female. Greenacre (1950) suggests that such a dichotomy may normally develop during the phallic period. If so, then for the girl to see her genitals as partly male and partly female may be a typical and perhaps transitory part of the gender differentiation process.

A third issue concerns the relationship between clitoral and vaginal experience, particularly if it has been dichotomized. In Freud's view clitoral and vaginal experience do not normally occur together. The former is normal in childhood; transition to the latter occurs in adolescence or adulthood. If, as current evidence suggests, both vagina and clitoris (more accurately, female genitalia as whole) are within the young girl's experience, exploration is invited of the integration and differentiation of these two foci of her genital experience. Distinctive fantasies or identity patterns may be elaborated in relation to each. Relationships may be established between them, for instance, in masturbatory ritual. Experience related to each may be split off from one another.

A fourth issue concerns the developmental fate of the dichotomization. In Freud's view it is anatomically based and permanent. The proposed framework suggests that normally the girl's genitals as a whole are integrated into her body image as girl. If so, the persistence of dichotomization may signal disturbance in gender development. Freud suggests that clitoral genitality must be given up in childhood to avoid excessive masculinization. The proposed view suggests that in normal development clitoral genitality (in the context of genital experience as a whole) is not renounced but categorized as female. In Freud's view optimal development requires that the girl recognize herself as castrated. In the proposed view she recognizes herself as female.

A third dimension of the meaning of the term castration in the context of the girl's response to her recognition of sex difference has to do with what it is that is lost in 'castration.' Explicitly it is the loss of the penis. Freud says that the girl sees the penis, realizes that she doesn't have one, and wants it. Her sense is of having had it and lost it. Clinical observation has seemed to bear out Freud's notion of the potency of this experience. Various explanations have been given for the intensity of the girl's reaction: the penis is external and visible, it is more potent in urinating in a wide arc, it is handier for masturbation. None has been altogether satisfying.

Rado (1933) outlines the problem in a way that highlights the issues and is in tune with current observational evidence as well. The girl becomes aware that the boy has a penis, and she does so in a particular developmental context. Her interest in her genitals has intensified. She has begun to masturbate with pleasure. The awareness that the boy has a genital organ that she does not, cannot in itself reduce her possibilities of pleasure. The illusion that everybody is the same has been shaken but nothing actual has been taken away. Why, then, Rado asks, does the girl, in the context of her own satisfying experience react as if she has been castrated, has lost everything, is without a centrally important part of herself?

Some possible contributions to that reaction from the early differentiation period have been suggested earlier. But there is another. It is largely implicit in Freud's formulations. It suggests that what may give rise to the intense reactions of loss, emptiness, utter lack, and so forth, is the giving up of genital excitement *per se*. In Freud's writing this is only implicit but it is there: it is the sight of the penis that causes the reactions he suggests, but at this time the girl also turns away from genital pleasure. Deutsch (1930) makes a relevant observation but does not integrate it into her formulation. In her discussion of castration, penis envy, and masochism she points out that these developments occur when the girl gives up masturbation: as long as she gets pleasure from masturbation the masochistic development does not occur. Jones (1927) makes a relevant argument in his discussion of the psychological meaning of castration anxiety, suggesting that the term *aphanisis* be substituted, that what is feared is the loss of all genital pleasure. Fraiberg (1972) more recently suggests that patients' sense of loss typically understood as representative of penis envy, may instead reflect the girl's or woman's inhibition of genital excitement. These observations open the possibility that girls' intense loss reactions in the context of the recognition of sex difference occur not as a result of seeing that boys have penises and they do not, but when (or if) they turn away from the genital pleasure that has become a satisfying part of their experience. In Freud's framework this alternative view can have no place. Childhood genital pleasure in his view is masculine. It is associated with the male genital organ. Normal feminine development requires that it be given up.

The differentiation framework suggests that the issue of giving up having a penis and giving up genital pleasure are separable. The developmentally appropriate involvement with issues of sex difference is signalled by the girl's awareness that boys have penises and girls do not. The favorable resolution of the differentiation process requires that she give up having a penis herself, and substitute for the notion of possession the elaboration of relationship between herself as female and the other as male. In favorable outcome she does *not* turn away from genital involvement. Instead, as part of her recategorization of her experience in gender terms, that involvement becomes categorized as specifically female. Freud sees the girl's turning away from genital involvement as not only normal but required for adequate feminine development. The differentiation framework suggests that such turning away represents a significant *failure* in gender differentiation.

DEVELOPMENTS IN FEMININITY

The proposed framework suggests that the girl's genital sexuality is central to the elaboration of her femininity. There is psychoanalytic literature in support of the proposed view. Jacobson (1976), in a paper first published in 1937, suggests that it is the girl's discovery of her own genitals that permits her to give up the notion of having a penis. Her libidinal cathexis of the vagina, her energetic investigation of her genitals and her masturbatory satisfaction contribute to the development of an active-genital relation to her sexual partner. Kestenberg (1968) speaks of the girl's sense of a 'productive inside' playing a role in her development. Erikson's (1965) studies of girls' and boys' play suggest that the girl, has a 'productive sense of inner space.' Torok (1970) emphasizes the importance of the girl's genital satisfaction in developing the capacity for orgasm and in establishing the groundwork of heterosexual competence.

The character of feminine genitality in adulthood is also different as seen in the two perspectives. In Freud's view normal femininity is passive. Abraham (1920) is explicit as to his use of the term, 'We must keep in view the fact that sexual activity is essentially associated with the male organ, that the woman is only in the position to excite the man's libido or respond to it, and that otherwise she is compelled to adopt a waiting attitude.' Deutsch (1944) emphasizes that the essence of femininity is a biologically based passivity and masochism. The vagina is a completely passive receptive organ that is entirely dependent on the man's activity. Feminine behavior is congruently passive and dependent. The erotic woman who has coped successfully with her masculinity is neither active towards nor independent of the man. She identifies with the man, feels herself a part of him, is a help-meet, is not active herself.

The proposed view suggests that the girl's genital satisfactions are an active bodily center of her developing femininity. Kestenberg's (1968) elaboration of notions of endogenous origins of femininity and on the girl's productive inside; Jacobson's (1976) emphasis on the girl's libidinal cathexis of her vagina and its contribution to an active-genital relationship to her partner; and Torok's (1970) focus on the girl's achievement of independent satisfaction in her genitality emphasize vigorous function rather than passivity.

Moreover, the femininity Freud asserts to be normal would from a differentiation perspective be seen as disturbed. Indications that a woman had no sense of her own productive genitality or of an elaboration of her own identity as feminine, no suggestion of a feeling of herself and the man independent of and in reciprocal relation to one another would suggest the persistence of influences from the early undifferentiated state. One would expect then that the reciprocal of these notions, that the man is all and she nothing, would also be in evidence: herself as narcissistically complete and the man as utterly lacking.

Jacobson (1976) attempts to alert the reader to such possibilities. She describes a type of woman who thoroughly fits Freud's notions of normal femininity. It becomes clear, however, that narcissistic residues pervade what appears to be her optimum relationship to the man. When the woman is in secure possession of him she functions well, but if loss threatens she reacts with pathological depression or other narcissistic disorder. It is these narcissistic reactions that suggest the underlying pathology. Actually, Jacobson suggests, such womens' genitality "is a sham since they experience the partner's genital as belonging to their own bodies." In normal development, "the phallic narcissism of the girl gives way to object libido." In the passive dependent femininity Freud considers to be normal, that development is incomplete.

The differentiation framework would suggest that the presence of such an incompletely differentiated feminine gender identity would be accompanied by disturbed notions of masculinity as well. Here again Freud's view and the proposed one differ. In Freud's view the woman is originally masculine in her experience. The question of her failing to understand masculinity does not easily arise. In the proposed view notions of *both* masculinity and femininity are products of the differentiation process and are developed reciprocally. Therefore, incomplete developments in the girl's patterning of femininity are likely to be matched by complementary narcissism in her notions of masculinity.

In the context of the woman's sense of herself as altogether without autonomous identity, the reciprocal notion that the male has 'everything' would be expected. Deutsch (1944) suggests it to be normal. The erotic woman, she suggests, lives with the notion, 'He is great and I am part of him.' From a differentiation perspective such a notion signals the possibility of disturbed relation to the man: intense disappointment and rage at any sign of flaw in the man's 'greatness'; assertion of narcissistic control over him; inability accurately to emphathize with either his disappointments or successes, the former being intolerable, the latter no more than to be expected.

In the context of her developing sense of her own femininity the girl's relations to her parents are altered. Freud suggests that the girl turns in disappointment and contempt from the mother to the father and thus from a homosexual to a heterosexual orientation. A wish for a child from the father substitutes for the wish for a penis.

The differentiation framework suggests that as the girl recategorizes her experience in gender terms changes occur in her relations to each parent. She now learns to relate to each parent in specifically gender terms. She learns to relate to her mother as a same-sex person, to identify with her without losing self-other differentiation, to maintain an object relationship without the intrusion of notions of narcissistic unity. She must learn to relate to the father now as specifically male in relation to her own self as female. These new orientations provide contexts within which she practices and elaborates the differentiated notions of femininity and of masculinity she is developing.

It is in this context too that triadic relationships first become focal. Her cross-sex relation to her father is developed in the context of her same-sex relation to her mother. Her stance towards the mother is altered by the fact of a simultaneous cross-sex relation to her father. Both are needed anchors for a new independence: her relation to the father provides a needed separateness from the mother as she elaborates her identifications with and same-sex relationship to her. The relation to the mother is an independent source of support for her femininity as she develops her cross-sex relation to her father as masculine. The wish for a child epitomizes the triadic situation: the wish for a baby simultaneously expresses both the identification with the mother as female and the heterosexual relation to the father as male.

Here too, characteristics of women that Freud views as normally feminine seem from a differentiation point of view to signal disturbance. For the girl to turn away from the mother in anger and disappointment for not giving her a penis and in contempt for all things feminine, suggests characteristics of that early stage in differentiation when the notion of self as complete and other as lacking alternates with the reverse: the mother is seen as both totally powerful in her ability to give the girl a penis, and utterly lacking in being a castrate herself.

To turn towards the father in the context of this repudiation of the mother seems also to represent disturbance: a displacement rather than a differentiation. Freud's (1933) further characterization of the relationship supports that notion. The father in such cases is seen as haven or refuge. The relationship to him is in virtually all respects identical to the prior relation to the mother. His love substitutes for the narcissistic wound of not having a penis. In adult life the woman may choose a man who represents her own ideal of what she would have been had she been a man.

To wish for a baby from the father as substitute for the penis, a compensation for organ inferiority rather than in elaboration of the triadic relationship, seems similarly to signal incomplete differentiation. A persisting sense of organ inferiority suggests that the woman's sense of her own independent and vigorous genitality is poorly established. If the child substitutes for a penis which represents unlimited potential, the woman may anticipate utter perfection in the child, and with its birth a renewal of her own sense of unlimited potential and completeness. The potential for difficulties in such circumstances is evident. As Torok (1970) points out, a child that substitutes for a penis can only feel that the mother wants to keep it forever as an appendage, the mother in turn that she must keep her children attached to her or lapse into bitterness and envy.

SUMMARY

Gender *differentiation* is proposed as a model for understanding aspects of gender development. The differentiation process is hypothesized to be patterned in ways similar to those of other major developmental differentiations (e.g., self-other, subjective and objective reality, intention and physical causality): an initial narcissistic, undifferentiated period; recognition of limits with response of protest, sense of loss, denial, and so on; a recategorization of experience in which one differentiation product is integrated as part of self, the other recognized to be independent of self, the two in productive relationship. Freud's major observations of feminine development are explored in differentiation terms: the period prior to awareness of sex difference; the recognition of sex difference; further developments in femininity. The differential implications of Freud's interpretation of these observations and of the one proposed are examined.

REFERENCES

Abraham, K. (1920). Manifestations of the female castration complex. In K. Abraham, *Selected Papers on Psychoanalysis*. New York: Basic Books, 1927.

Bettelheim, B. (1954). *Symbolic Wounds*. Glencoe, Illinois: The Free Press.

Deutsch, H. (1930). The significance of masochism in the mental life of women. *Int. J. Psycho-Anal.* **11:** 48–60.

Deutsch, H. (1933). Motherhood and sexuality. *Psychoanal. Q.* **2:** 476–488.

Deutsch, H. (1944). *The Psychology of Women: Vol. 1*. New York: Grune & Stratton.

Erikson, E. H. (1965). Inner and outer space: reflections on womanhood. In Robert J. Lifton (ed.), *The Woman in America*. Houghton-Mifflin.

Fraiberg, S. (1972). Some characteristics of genital arousal and discharge in latency girls. *Psychoanal. Study Child* **27.**

Freud, S. (1923). The ego and the id. *S.E.* **19.**

Freud, S. (1933). New introductory lectures on psychoanalysis: XXXIII Femininity. *S.E.* **22.**

Freud, S. (1937). Analysis terminable and interminable. *S.E.* **23.**

Galenson, E. & Roiphe, H. (1977). Some suggested revisions concerning early female development. In H. P. Blum (ed.), *Female Psychology*. New York: Int. Univ. Press.

Greenacre, P. (1950). Special problems of early female sexual development. *Psychoanal. Study Child.* **5.**

Jacobson, E. (1976). Ways of female superego formation and the female castration conflict. *Psychoanal. Q.* **45:** 525–538.

Jones, E. (1927). The early development of female sexuality. *Int. J. Psycho-Anal.* **8:** 459–472.

Kestenberg, J. S. (1968). Outside and inside, male and female. *J. Am. psychoanal. Ass.* **16:** 457–520.

Kubie, L. S. (1974). The drive to become both sexes. *Psychoanal. Q.* **43:** 349–426.

Kleeman, J. A. (1977). Freud's views on early female sexuality in the light of direct child observation. In H. P. Blum (ed.), *Female Psychology.* New York: Int. Univ. Press.

Parens, H., Pollack, L., Stern, J. & Kramer, S. (1977). On the girl's entry into the Oedipus complex. In H. P. Blum (ed.), *Female Psychology.* New York: Int. Univ. Press.

Rado, W. (1933). Fear of castration in women. *Psychoanal. Q.* **2:** 425–475.

Stoller, R. J. (1968). *Sex and Gender.* New York: Aronson.

Torok, M. (1970). The significance of penis envy in women. In Chasseguet-Smirgel (ed.), *Female Sexuality: New Psychoanalytic Views.* Ann Arbor: Univ. Mich. Press.

3 Gender Differentiation in Boys

INTRODUCTION

Freud's theory of gender development in girls has been the focus of vigorous re-assessment from the time of its first publication. No such intensive and critical review has been directed at his conceptualization of the development of masculinity in boys. However, an examination of that theory suggests that its problems are equally severe and that they center around the same persistend difficulty. Specifically, the difficulty is in providing a theoretical perspective for understanding the interplay of masculinity and femininity in the developing personality.

Freud's thinking produced two conceptual frameworks for understanding that interplay in men. The first is his theory of bisexuality and the second his conceptualization of the development of masculinity in boys. Each offers formulations about major aspects of gender development: the biological substrate, the developmental period prior to awareness of sex difference (bisexuality theory proposes no formulation here), the developments attendant on the boy's becoming aware of sex difference, and the processes of the oedipal period. However, the two theories are incompatible. They have contradictory implications for every one of these points in the boy's development.

Moreover, neither is acceptable in its present form. Available biological evidence does not support Freud's notion of a biologically determined bisexuality. Bisexuality in men is observed clinically, however, and Freud's development theory cannot occommodate such observations. Neither can the developmental theory find a place for notions, now generally accepted, of boys' early identifications with their mothers.

This chapter explores aspects of boys' gender development as a gender differentiation process. The conceptual aim is to accommodate the observations subsumed under both Freud's theories of boys' gender development in a single framework, and to do so without doing violence to currently accepted biological and developmental knowledge. Some implications of this conceptualization are elaborated for the phenomena of one developmental phase, the consequences for the boy of becoming aware of sex difference. This is the point at which gender differentiation is hypothesized as beginning. In Freud's view this recognition is salient for the boy's belief that sex difference can be equated with having or not having a penis, the occurrence of sex-difference related castration anxiety, the defensive denial of sex difference in notions of the phallic mother, and the emergence of the meanings of masculinity as active and sadistic, and femininity as passive and masochistic. The phenomena underlying each of these formulations are reexamined from the perspective of gender differentiation.

CONCEPTUAL FRAMEWORKS: FREUD'S THEORIES (BISEXUALITY AND GENDER DEVELOPMENT) AND THE GENDER DIFFERENTIATION PERSPECTIVE

Freud's Theories of Bisexuality and of Gender Development in Boys

The interplay of the male and female in the individual was of prime importance to Freud from the time of his early correspondence with Fliess (Freud, 1896, p. 238). His observations of men's bisexuality seemed undeniable to him. Men could regularly be observed to have wishes to take the woman's role in sexual intercourse, to be impregnated by a man, to bear a child, and to be involved in the birth process. These themes could be seen to exist side by side with masculine orientations. This duality of masculine and feminine tendencies could be observed in dreams (Freud, 1900, p. 359), in masturbatory ceremony (Freud, 1908), and in symptom formation (Freud, 1908). Freud perceived men's feminine strivings as contributing to the intensity of castration anxiety attendant on the recognition of sex difference and accounting for the negative Oedipus complex (Freud, 1908, p. 6 [Editor's Note]).

Nevertheless, Freud was not able to conceptualize bisexuality in developmental terms. As he looked back over his work toward the end of his professional life (Freud, 1940), it seemed to him that bisexuality had defied his every effort to trace its developmental course. It must be consigned wholly to the province of biology. Men's feminine strivings, he concluded, have to do with a constitutionally based bisexual disposition. Their wishes to bear children are founded in biology. The anxiety-arousing press of feminine wishes when sex difference becomes focal is constitutionally based. The assumption of a female role in the context of the negative Oedipus complex, is an expression of the feminine aspect of a universally present, biologically based sexual duality.

Concurrently, however, Freud was elaborating his theory of gender development in boys. In this theory, boys' biological dispositions, their reaction to the recognition of sex difference, and the nature of their Oedipus complex are seen in quite different terms. This conceptualization has a very limited place in boys' development, for the feminine. It almost exclusively emphasizes the male and masculine.

In this formulation all developmental influences in the boy's pre-oedipal period are seen as tending toward the establishment of his masculinity. Anatomically, the boy is male. His instinctual aims, when they arise in the phallic period, are masculine. His first relationship (to his mother), by its cross-sex character, predisposes him to heterosexuality. In his experience there is only one sex, the male one. He uncritically assumes that everyone is, like himself, altogether male and masculine. To him sex difference means only possessing or not possessing a penis. When the boy sees that the girl has no penis he assumes that she had one and lost it. Castration anxiety expresses the fear that it might happen to him as well.

The Oedipus complex occurs when the boy begins to feel rivalry and hostility toward the father in relation to his passionate interest in the mother and his wish for exclusive possession of her. The relation to the mother, already heterosexual from the period of earliest attachment, remains unaltered. The central oedipal struggles take place between the boy and his father. They are resolved when, in the context of castration anxiety, the boy gives up his rivalry with the father, identifies with him, and in the acceptance of his values takes a major step in the consolidation of his superego.

These two formulations, the theories of bisexuality and of gender development, are central to the psychoanalytic conception of gender development in men. They are incompatible in significant ways. In one, all biological influences on gender development are posited to be male and to dispose the boy to masculinity. In the other, a biologically-based femininity has an important place. In one, the boy assumes everyone to be, like himself, male. In the other, the boy himself has constitutionally based masculine and feminine tendencies. In one, sex difference, to the boy, means only the possession or lack of a penis. In the other, the boy's recognition of sex difference includes awareness of feminine wishes that he must suppress. In one, recognition of sex difference involves becoming aware only of *another's* lack. In the other, it includes the boy's renunciation of *his own* wishes. In one, the attendant castration anxiety represents the boy's fear that he, like the girl, might lose his penis. In the other, it has two roots, the fear of losing his penis by castration, or as a result of failing to give up his wishes for femaleness. In one, his first genital orientation is entirely male. In the other it ranges over both the male and the female before, typically, moving definitively toward maleness and masculinity.

Toward a Reconceptualization of Gender Development in Boys

New data and altered perspectives within psychoanalytic psychology suggest directions for an integrative reformulation. The best currently available physiological knowledge suggests that to the extent that anatomy and physiology influence the boy's gender development they do so in the direction of masculinity (Stoller, 1968). That is, available evidence does not support Freud's notion of a biologically based femininity in boys. The occurrence of boys' wishes to bear children, to take the woman's role in sexual intercourse, or to be impregnated, cannot be accepted as biological givens—a female tendency matched by a male one to form a constitutionally based duality. Social and intra-individual bases must be sought for the presence of both masculine and feminine orientations in boys and to account for their interplay and development course.

Possible bases for a social and developmental formulation exist in broadly accepted data and perspectives concerning the boy's earliest development. It is well-documented that from the time of sex ascription at birth the boy's caregiving environment (perhaps centrally the mother but certainly also the father) treats him in ways that foster his development in the direction of his society's notions of masculinity (Mead, 1967; Stoller, 1968; Block, 1977). Within psychoanalytic psychology it is now generally accepted that the father plays a significant role in the boy's early development (e.g., Ross, 1977), and that with respect to the mother the boy not only forms a relationship that predisposes him to heterosexuality but also forms a broad range of identifications, among them identification with her in her capacity for child bearing.

The notion of the boy's early identification with the mother in the context of a generally masculine development offers the possibility of a developmental framework for the sexual duality Freud observed. If the boy develops in a masculine direction but also, by identifying with his mother, assumes for himself attributes of his mother that cannot be his (among them her procreative capacities) then the groundwork is laid for an interplay of the masculine and feminine in his personality.

Freud's developmental theory of the boy's gender development cannot accommodate the notion of the boy's early identification with the mother. Every major tenet of that theory is called into question by it. If the boy has made identifications with his mother in her procreative capacity a part of his self structure then sex difference means more to him than the presence or absence of a penis. He is not aware of only one sex, the male one, but also of a female one whose characteristics he admires but must forego. Hence, the anxiety attendant on sex difference does not (or not solely) concern loss of his penis but includes the loss of the potential for female attributes he has assumed for himself. Furthermore, the oedipal period involves not only male rivalry for possession of the mother but the boy's establishment of himself as masculine in relation to both his parents who are now newly perceived in terms of their gender.

An integrative reformulation of Freud's theory of male gender development is both required and made possible by taking seriously the notion of the boy's early identification with the mother. It is required because Freud's developmental theory cannot in its present form accommodate it. It is made possible because its inclusion permits conceptualization of a developmental base for bisexuality.

Gender Development as a Differentiation Process

In Chapter 2 processes of gender differentiation in girls are placed in the context of other developments out of previously undifferentiated (narcissistic) experience. These same differentiation parameters can be applied to boys' gender development. The gender differentiation perspective posits that the boy's earliest gender experience is undifferentiated. Objectively the boy's anatomy is male and to the extent that physiological processes are influential they dispose him toward masculinity. From the time of birth the caretaking environment behaves toward him in ways that encourage his development in a masculine direction. However, his subjective sense of himself is not yet limited by the realities of his actual sex. He has no sense of a differentiated sex and gender. His sense of himself includes all possibilities, ones he will come to categorize as male and as female, now however, occurring in an undifferentiated array.

In this perspective current biological knowledge that boys are male in anatomy and physiological disposition is taken into account. Early identifications with the mother find a place. Dispositions to both masculinity and femininity are posited, not as distinct tendencies but in an as yet undifferentiated array. Although the boy is not considered to be male and masculine in all respects, he is assumed to have made major developments in a masculine direction. It is his *understanding* of what may be included in his sense of himself as boy (an identification he is able to make at about two years of age) that is over-extended, not yet limited by the realities of sex differences.

As with other differentiations, gender ifferentiation is hypothesized to begin with the recognition of a limit. It begins as the boy gradually becomes increasingly aware of the meanings of sex difference. He notices that some capacities and attributes (expressed in self representations or as identifications) that he had assumed for himself cannot be his. They are the prerogatives of women. The genital difference between males and females determines the limits he must recognize. His typical reaction, is a sense of loss or deprivation although objectively no loss of attributes or capacities has occurred. However, the loss is actual, in that self representations embodying desired capacities and attributes must be given up as possibilities for himself. He may respond with protest, denial of sex difference, and so forth. Such reactions are usually transient.

In this framework the meaning of sex difference for the boy is more than the presence or lack of a penis. Sex difference means a move from the narcissistic assumption that all sex and gender characteristics are open to him, to a recognition of the limits imposed by the reality of his body's structure and function. His feeling of loss is not responsive to perception of another's loss, but of his own. To be female does not mean (at this point) to be castrated, but to have admired attributes he cannot have. His related anxieties are not (or not only) castration anxiety (fears for the loss of his penis). They also involve the giving up of potentialities that he now perceives to be female. Relinquishing such possibilities does not involve suppression of a biologically based femininity but abandoning of self representations acquired by identification.

As in the case of other major developmental differentiations the processes subsequent to recognition of limit involve the differentiation of the boy's experience into complementary categories. Out of the undifferentiated array of self representations (labelled 'boy') a new masculinity and femininity begin to be differentiated. They are elaborated as complementary categories, each being defined in relation to the other, each beginning to have its own validity, each becoming distinct from the other. The boy elaborates masculinity within himself, centered in his male body. Femininity is attributed to members of the other sex, centered in their female bodies. "Boy" begins to assume new meanings. Rather than a label applied to himself that subsumes the entire undifferentiated mass of his self experience, it gradually becomes a delimited and articulated gender-specific concept defined in relation to its other-sex complement. The female and feminine is increasingly recognized as belonging to members of the other sex, neither part of the boy nor in his possession, but accessible to him in relationship. In other words, the narcissistic elaboration of masculinity and femininity within the self is replaced by its elaboration in object relations.

This formulation proposes that the boy does not normally continue to assume that there is only one sex, the male one. The character of his masculinity does not continue relatively unchanged but is re-defined. His notions of what it means to be female involve more than "no penis." Recognition of sex difference normally does not result in his holding the female in contempt as a castrate but recognition that he must attribute to her valued capacities not present in himself. His notions of masculinity and femininity are not predetermined by biological dispositions (though physiological factors may have some influence on the patterning of his masculinity) but are differentiated out of the array of his self representations. The boy does not typically continue to elaborate his experience of masculinity and femininity within himself, but instead does so within relationships.

The processes of the oedipal period continue the differentiation process. They provide the arena for the boy to test and elaborate his notions of masculinity and of femininity in his relations to his father and his mother. His father is viewed now as specifically masculine, his mother perceived as specifically feminine in terms of his developing meanings of these terms. They provide the major reality context (along with other adults, children, books, television, etc.) in which the boy can play out every possibility of same-sex and cross-sex relationships as he moves toward the firm establishment of his sex and gender categorizations. These categories usually take the form of the boy being masculine in same-sex relationships to men and cross-sex ones to women. In rivalries, identifications, and other interactions with his father he develops both his own masculinity and the possibilities of same-sex relationships. In relationships with his mother he tests and develops his notions of femininity as he views his mother in light of his increasingly articulated category of femininity. In his cross-sex relation to her he begins to work out his notions of the complementary relationships of masculinity and femininity. These processes are given added intensity because they occur in the context of the knowledge that she has female characteristics he has had to give up as possibilities for himself. They become more complex as they are worked out in the context of the boy's relation to his father and his parents' relationships to one another.

In this view he does not enter the oedipal period altogether male and masculine, and heterosexual in orientation. These are developments of the oedipal period itself. His perceptions of his father and mother do not remain largely unaltered but are newly defined in gender terms. The boy's trying out of sex role relationships is not limited to two: a feminine position in relation to the father as masculine (the negative Oedipus complex), and the masculine position of rivalry with the father for possession of the mother (the positive Oedipus complex). All possible roles and relationships to father and to mother are tried out on the way to the boy's final internal arrangements. Neither the relationships implied by the term 'negative Oedipus complex' nor any other are biologically determined. The boy's identification with the father and his values is not solely a reaction of defeat or capitulation in the face of castration threat. It is a part of the differentiation process. His relation to his mother, *objectively* heterosexual since birth, becomes so *in his experience* during this period.

IMPLICATIONS FOR ISSUES ATTENDANT ON THE INITIAL RECOGNITION OF SEX DIFFERENCE

Some implications of hypothesizing a gender-undifferentiated period prior to awareness of sex difference have been elaborated in the two earlier chapters. The consequences of gender differentiation theory for the complexities of the oedipal period are reserved for later discussion. With one exception (concerning the boy's identification with the mother in the period before gender differentiation), the aim here is limited to an exploration of some of the implications of gender differentiation theory for understanding the phenomena related to the boy's recognition of sex difference per se. In Freud's perspectives these include the influences of sexual duality, castration anxiety, denial of sex difference in the fantasy of the phallic mother, and the emergence of the meanings of masculinity and femininity as active-passive and sadistic-masochistic. Each of these issues is reformulated in gender differentiation terms with emphasis on the provision of a unified perspective to replace Freud's two disparate ones, the place of the boy's early identifications with the mother, and the way in which the interplay of masculinity and femininity is conceptualized.

Illustrative material is drawn primarily from Freud's own case presentations and from the perversion literature. The latter is particularly useful because perverse development in men is generally thought to be related to issues of sex difference. Moreover, because the available literature is rich in clinical observation it is possible to explore, in a preliminary way, the usefulness of differentiation concepts as an organizing framework in comparison to those generally used in the context of Freud's developmental and bisexuality theories.

The Boy Before Gender Differentiation: Proto-masculine, Feminine or Undifferentiated

Gender differentiation theory suggests that this early period provides bases for the development of both masculinity and femininity in the boy. It does not exclusively encourage the development of masculinity as Freud suggests. Nor is it usefully conceptualized as a feminine period in the boy, as others have proposed more recently.

The strongest argument for proposing that the earliest period in the boy's gender development be viewed as undifferentiated rather than tending exclusively toward masculinity, concerns observations of the boy's early identifications with his mother. Of these, his identifications with her in her child-bearing possibilities has been most extensively explored. If such identifications are not initially categorized in gender terms but are later perceived by the boy to represent female qualities antithetical to his maleness, then the early period is better conceptualized as undifferentiated than as tending exclusively toward masculinity.

It is generally accepted in psychoanalytic theory today that prior to recognition of sex difference the boy, in identification with his mother imagines himself able to give birth (e.g., Jacobson, 1950; Kleeman, 1966; Ross, 1977). Gender differentiation theory hypothesizes that this identification occurs in the context of a wide array of identifications initially not categorized as either male or female. It begins to be defined as female when the boy becomes aware of sex difference. At that time it may become involved in sex-difference conflict. Therefore, this early period is not appropriately conceptualized as exclusively protomasculine but as undifferentiated.

Freud's view (gender development theory) of the early period is different. In his view, too the boy regularly develops wishes to have a baby in the period prior to awareness of sex difference. However, these wishes do not occur in identification with the mother nor are they in any significant way related to her. They are not categorized by the boy as female wishes initially or subsequently. They play no part in the conflicts related to the boy's recognition of sex difference. When, in clinical work, notions of giving birth anally occur to men, these are representations of the later negative Oedipus complex now regressively expressed. Boys' wishes to give birth are of little theoretical or clinical significance. Their existence is no way contravenes the notion that boys' early development tends exclusively toward masculinity.

The strength of Freud's commitment to this view as well as indications that it is too limited a perspective, are evident in his three case histories of male patients, familiarly known as Little Hans (Freud, 1909a), the Rat Man (Freud, 1909b), and the Wolf Man (Freud, 1918). In each of the three, one contributor to the central symptom (the horse phobia, the rat fantasy, the phobic reaction to the wolf illustration) is the patient's notion that men can give birth to babies. In each case this fact enters Freud's discussion but is not found to be of particular dynamic significance.

In the case discussions of Little Hans and the Wolf Man additional relevant data are reported. Hans' phobia is related in time to the birth of his sister. It occurs in the context of his explicit assertions that both he and his father can have babies, his intensive and protracted fantasy play with "his children," his admission to his father that whenever he has a bowel movement he imagines himself to be making babies. In the phobia of horses the fallen, kicking, and heaving horse represents his mother in childbirth and the particularly frightening dray horses with heavily loaded vans symbolize his pregnant mother.

However, though Freud made these interpretations and reported them he did not perceive Hans' notions about giving birth as contributing significantly to his conflict. In his view, Hans' conflicts did not concern identifications with his mother. Hans' wishes to bear a child were not wishes for capacities that as a male he must give up as possibilities for himself. His conflict was related solely to his father. His sense of something broken or hurt represented only the possible retaliative loss of his penis and not the necessary relinquishing of the possibility of his bearing children.

In the case of the Wolf Man, Freud's exclusion of the boy's wishes for a baby as important in gender-relevant conflict is even more sharply delineated. In this presentation Freud's explicit focus is sex-difference, the boy's recognition that to be male he must give up desirable possibilities of femaleness. The phobic object of the young boy is a picture of a wolf. He remembers it as illustrating the story of either Little Red Riding Hood or the Wolf and the Seven Goats. The wolf is clearly masculine but in both stories also has living beings in his belly (the grandmother, the kids). The dream precipitating the phobia occurs on the eve of the boy's birthday, which is also Christmas Eve. (The question of God's, Joseph's, and Mary's roles in the birth of Jesus becomes a theme in his later obsessional neurosis). The dream concerns a Christmas tree on whose branches are presents. The presents are wolves with rear halves that are reminiscent of foxes with glorious tails (males). The fronts are like the sheep dogs at a sheep breeding farm. (Their caretaking function suggests femaleness, though Freud's focus is the boy's probable observation of sheep copulating at the farm, specifically the male mounting the female.)

In this case, too, though Freud elaborates these issues concerning the capacity to give birth and perceives that they are represented in the dream and the phobia he does not recognize them as having dynamic significance. Nor does he see them as occurring in identification with the mother. Rather, in Freud's view, they are evidence of the boy's unconflicted belief that men as well as women can have babies. Freud's focus is the boy's recognition, represented in the dream and resulting in the phobia, that he must give up femaleness if he is to be male. But giving birth is not included as a central part of femaleness, nor is femaleness related to the mother. The only femaleness is the boy's wish to take the woman's role in copulation with the father, with a subsidiary willingness to give him a baby, or wish to receive one from him.

These clinical observations (though not the conceptual formulations) are congruent with gender differentiation theory. They suggest that issues of child-bearing may be of clinically significant importance in the disturbances of boys and men. The historical link of Hans' difficulties to his mother's pregnancy suggests that his notions of child-bearing occurred in identification with the mother; not (or not solely) in relation to the father. In the case of the Wolf Man the recognition that child-bearing is a female capacity incompatible with his maleness seems to be focal in his dream, phobia, and later obsessional ruminations. If it can be accepted that boys do perceive child-bearing to be a female capacity when they become aware of sex difference, and that pregnancy and childbirth do become dynamically significant sex difference issues, then the boy's development prior to awareness of sex difference is more usefully construed to be undifferentiated than to be masculine.

The more recent general recognition that boys' wishes to bear children occur in identification with their mothers has led others to the hypothesis that in the boy a feminine phase precedes his entry into the phallic period. Boehm (1930) suggested the existence of such a phase, though he viewed it as the boy's femininity in relation to the father, not the mother. As he put it, the male is first a little girl and, after castration anxiety, a boy. Kestenberg (1956) suggests the existence in the boy of an "inner genital phase" that must be repudiated for the boy to enter the phallic phase. Bell (1964) posits a testicular phase involving feminine identifications prior to the phallic phase. Stoller (1968), focusing on the boy's feminine identifications rooted in his first encounters with his mother's female body and feminine qualities, emphasizes that the boy must dis-identify [Greenson's term (1968)] with the mother in order to establish a masculine identity.

For these early identifications with the mother appropriately to be called part of a feminine phase there must be some grouping, however primitive, of identifications characterized as feminine, juxtaposed to a masculinity in some measure distinct from it. There is little observational material that bears directly on this issue. Available theory would speak against it. It suggests that this phase occurs prior to the boy's focal awareness of sex difference and therefore before the grouping of gender-related identifications with sex difference as the focus has been made. Moreover, as Buttenheim (1979) points out, to postulate a feminine phase in the boy ignores (or denies) the boy's concurrent developments in the direction of masculinity. The interaction (or lack of it) between the boy's masculinity and the postulated femininity is not discussed. Generally it is suggested only that the boy must renounce or pass beyond the feminine one toward the masculine orientation of the phallic phase.

Gender differentiation theory posits istead that this period prior to awareness of sex difference is neither masculine nor feminine. Self-representations that lay the groundwork for *both* masculinity and femininity are developed during this period. They are not yet organized into gender categories. That organization is a developmental achievement.

Sexual Duality: Biological Given or Developmental Accomplishment

Bisexuality or sexual duality implies that some aspects of the individual are characterized as masculine, others as feminine. The masculine ones are integrated into one organization, the feminine ones into another. Gender differentiation theory proposes that bisexuality in the boy is developmentally based. The boy's notions of both masculinity and femininity are products of a differentiation process that begins when the boy becomes focally aware of sex difference.

Several implications differentiate this formulation from Freud's notion of a biologically based and patterned sexual duality. In Freud's view the emerging feminine themes in the boy centrally concern the wish to take a passive female role in copulation with the father, but may also be expressions of the boy's wish for a baby from him. In the gender differentiation perspective they represent a newly developing category based on early identifications. Notions of bearing a child occur in identification with the mother, not (or not solely) in relation to the father. They represent ideas of power and productivity not passivity. Masculinity, in Freud's view, is a biologically determined active and sadistic force centered in the male genitals. Viewed as a differentiation product, it is seen to be patterned on early experience, and the secure establishment of the male genitals as its bodily center is a developmental accomplishment achieved with varying degrees of success. In Freud's view masculinity and femininity in the man are disparate themes in their constitutional origins, and when feminine wishes occur with significant strength in males they represent wishes to be a woman *instead of* a man. Differentiation theory suggests that masculinity and femininity in men are originally not distinct themes. Their differentiation is a developmental task whose successful completion is not assured. The persistence of feminine themes in the man represents his reluctance to give up the possibilities of femaleness. He wishes to have all sex and gender possibilities, to be *both* masculine and feminine.

The perversion literature offers possibilities for exploring aspects of these differential predictions. Although the conceptual frameworks in the published discussions tend to involve notions of the phallic mother and of bisexuality in Freud's sense, the reported observations appear to be congruent with differentiation theory.

Patients' fantasies about child-bearing are regularly noted. They appear to represent admired capacities not passive orientations. Their roots in development can frequently be observed or inferred with some degree of certainty. Their link to the mother is often explicitly related to her pregnancy. Khan (1965), for example, describes a fetishistic patient whose behavior with his fetish is interpreted as representing wishes to give birth. These wishes are linked to his childhood experience of his mother's pregnancy and are admired capacities without which the patient felt "maimed." Socarides (1960) describes a patient with perversions, whose mother gave birth in his fourth year and whose own related yearnings to give birth were elaborated during adolescence in the repetitive staging of puppet plays whose explicit theme was child-bearing, and during adulthood in fantasies such as ones in which "a good strong man" becomes pregnant. Sperling (1964) analyzes the emergence of transvestite tendencies in a young boy after the birth of a child in his home. His wishes for femininity are vividly expressed in dreams and fantasies of everyone being half girl and half boy, or of himself possessing a magic liquid or magic clothes that enable the owner to change sex at will.

These wishes do not appear to represent desires to be a woman *instead of* a man but a reluctance to give up the possibilities of *both*. Sperling's child patient wanted to be half girl and half boy, and to have magic options to be either. Socarides' patient imagined "a good strong man" becoming pregnant. Khan's patient saw in a penis with a foreskin the inseparable oneness of the masculinity and femininity for which he yearned.

The masculinity juxtaposed to or in conflict with such patients' wishes for femininity is not a biologically based, masterful, sadistic force centered in the genitals. Weaknesses in the patient's masculinity are regularly described. Usually they are discussed as interferences in the man's masculinity due to feminine identifications and castration anxiety, not as failures in masculine development per se. Greenacre (1968), however, explicitly suggests a vulnerability in the patient's masculinity due to a developmental failure in the consolidation of his male genital body image.

There are hints, finally, that in some cases the gender categorization itself is incomplete. Bak (1968), for example, observes that in cases of perversion the man has not developed a clear demarcation of the sexes. He suggests that in perverse activity the major thrill may be unity and fusion with the mother who is perceived to be female and to have male genitals as well. Greenacre (1968), similarly, suggests that in cases of fetishism the man has a continuing sense of confusion and fluidity in his notion of his body parts. Thus, rather than a feminine theme in conflict with a biologically rooted male one, Bak and Greenacre suggest that the patient's sense of a differentiated masculinity and femininity can itself be deficient.

These observations support the notion that bisexuality is a developmental achievement rather than a biological given, that both masculinity and femininity are rooted in a prior undifferentiated state and are differentiation products. In men with sex difference related problems a significant issue may be the incomplete establishment of a genitally centered masculine identity, not only the fear of loss of an already prized center of their maleness. Issues of femininity may involve men's reluctance to relinquish prized capacities assumed for themselves in identification with their mothers, rather than passive wishes for their fathers. Wishes for femaleness may not be wishes to be a woman rather than a man, but men's regressive refusal to recognize the limits imposed by their actual sex.

Castration Anxiety: Loss of Maleness or of Femaleness

Gender differentiation theory proposes that the "castration anxiety" attendant on the boy's recognition of sex difference concerns the boy's sense of loss or deprivation in relation to femaleness, particularly represented in the mother's childbearing capacities. When he becomes aware of sex difference the boy begins to categorize his experience in gender terms. He begins to recognize that he must give up for himself the characteristics he defines as exclusively feminine. This loss is a real one. The boy must renounce those possibilities, which in the course of early identifications he included among his self representations. The focus of his sense of loss is his mother. She has what he must forego. His reaction is likely to include protest against the deprivations and envy of the woman who has what he lacks.

The predictions about sex difference related castration anxiety derived from this conceptualization differ sharply from Freud's. In Freud's view the boy's concern is for the loss of his penis, not of female capacities. The boy observes a lack in the girl (her castrated state), not that she has capacities denied him. His reaction to the other sex is derogation, not envy. As castration anxiety concerns wishes for female capacities they are biologically based wishes to be copulated with by the father, not psychologically elaborated ones based on identification with the mother. Giving up female wishes is not in itself a source of anxiety except insofar as retaining them threatens his penis.

Freud's observations of Little Hans and of the Wolf Man support the notion that in addition to the boy's fears for his penis in the context of hostile rivalry with his father (Little Hans) or wishes for a female relationship to the father incompatible with his masculinity (the Wolf Man), another context for "castration" anxiety exists. Hans' anxieties symbolized in phobic reactions to the fallen horse and the loaded van concern the child-bearing capacities of his mother. The Wolf Man's anxieties represented in the bisexual phobic object, the dream figures with female as well as male attitudes, and the later obsessional concerns about God's, Mary's, and Joseph's roles in the birth of Jesus, suggests a reluctance to believe that being masculine requires giving up possibilities of child-bearing.

The perversion literature also suggests that the sex difference related loss feelings in men refer to the loss of female capacities and the focus is the woman who is not so deprived. In Socarides' fetishistic patient castration anxiety was expressed in horror of open wounds and operations and was related to the patient's pregnancy fantasies, his repeated observation in childhood of his mother's Caesarian section scar, and his fantasies in which the pregnant "good strong man" must be cut open to get the baby out. Khan's patient's sense of 'maimed' masculinity concerned the loss of femaleness symbolized by loss of his foreskin, and his fetishistic behavior expressed his rage at his mother and his fear of masochistic surrender to her. Gillespie (1952) and Greenacre (1953) report observations of male patients whose use of fetishes and mode of sexual intercourse allowed them to imagine that they were taking over the woman's genital equipment.

These anxieties are generally referred to as castration anxieties. Their symbolic expression in horror of blood, wounds, and/or things lost or missing, are typical of those interpreted as castration anxiety. The loss, however, is not of the penis but of femaleness. The femaleness concerns birth-giving and female genitals, not (or not centrally) being copulated with by the father. The protest, the attempt at restitution (e.g., in getting the woman's genital equipment) or the rage is directed toward the woman as depriver, not toward the man.

If these observations are validated in further investigation it may be useful to distinguish two patterns of "castration" anxiety in men. An earlier one stems from issues of sex difference. A later one is centered in oedipal rivalry with the father. In the first, the loss ("castration") refers to female capacities, in the second, to male ones. In the first, the focal object (castrator) is the mother who has what the boy lacks; in the second, the castrator is the father who retaliates against the boy for his hostile wishes. In the first, the major associated affects are envy, spite, and derogation; in the second, hostile rivalry. In clinical observation where both may be present, the momentary or prevailing predominance of one pattern over the other may provide useful clues to other relevant issues. It may be helpful in determining whether the salient concern is one of sex difference or oedipal rivalry, maternal or paternal transferences, loss or damage anxieties related to reluctance to give up bisexual completeness or to loss of maleness.

Defense Against Recognition of Sex Difference: Fantasy of Phallic Mother or of Bisexual Completeness

Denial of sex difference is recognized to be a major defense against the anxieties (castration anxiety) attendant on accepting it. In Freud's view this denial is expressed in the notion of the phallic mother. Gender differentiation theory argues that it occurs in notions of bisexual completeness.

These predictions follow directly from theory differences. In Freud's view the boy, prior to awareness of sex difference, is entirely male and masculine in orientation. He knows of only one sex, the male one. He has no notion of a distinctively female body. (His notions of giving birth are modelled on the digestive process that does not require a body different than his own.) Recognition of sex differences involves only becoming aware that the woman has no penis (formulation in this regard is restricted to the developmental theory). In denial of sex difference he imputes a penis to her.

Differentiation theory proposes that prior to awareness of sex difference the boy uncritically assumes all sex and gender possibilities for himself. Sex difference means awareness that what is female cannot be his. Denial of sex difference occurs in the reassertion for himself of all sex and gender possibilities. Both what he now knows to be exclusively male and what he knows to be the prerogative of females remain his.

The perversion literature is particularly useful here in providing an arena for comparative evaluation of these two views. Since Freud's major contribution to understanding perversion (1927) the notion of the phallic mother has been conceptually central, and supporting observations have regularly been made. Gender differentiation theory predicts that notions of the phallic mother will be found in the context of notions of bisexual wholeness: that is, when the male patient attributes a penis to the mother he will attribute female qualities to her as well, and his notion of himself will also include both male and female attributes. Studies reported in the literature support these latter notions. Khan (1965) for example, describes his patient as attributing to his mother a phallus to avoid castration anxiety, but he also describes the patient as identifying with his mother as procreative. The patient himself expresses in his fetish the notion of maleness and femaleness in indissoluble union in one person as the ideal state. Socarides' (1960) patient believed that the woman has a hidden penis, but he also wished to bear a child as she could, and in his own fantasies a "good strong man" had the capacity to become pregnant. Bak (1968) also emphasizes the centrality of the notion of the female phallus in perversion, but this is not a phallus attributed to the mother to maintain the notion that she is male like himself. Rather, Bak suggests that the patient attributes a phallus to the mother without denial of the vagina and that he identifies with her. In such fantasy and identification the patient attributes bisexual wholeness to both his mother and himself.

Outside the perversion literature occasional relevant observations have been made as well. Lorand (1939) for example, suggested that men who retain the idea of the woman with a penis to avoid castration anxiety also attribute to men female genitals for the same purpose. Curiously, Freud also made a congruent observation though he did not pursue its conceptual implications. He remarked (1923) that in the course of development the boy's idea of the phallic mother disappears when he gives up the idea that men can have babies. In gender differentiation terms that observation would suggest that the boy gives up the idea that the mother has both femaleness and a phallus when he gives up the notion that he, a male person, also has female possibilities. That is, he can recognize that his mother is not bisexually whole when he gives up notions of bisexual completeness for himself.

Masculinity and Femininity: Activity and Passivity

In Freud's view masculinity and femininity are biologically patterned as active and passive respectively. To be active is to be the doer, to be passive the one done to. Activity-passivity is the central dichotomous theme of the anal period. In the genital period, following recognition of sex difference, activity and passivity become identified with masculinity and femininity. The boy's activity of the anal stage is expressed in large muscle activity, active mastery, and curiosity about the environment. This becomes integral to his masculinity in the genital stage. Freud does not specify the organization of passivity in the anal stage in a way complementary to the large muscle active mode. The femininity of the genital phase, however, is identified with passivity and seen to be organized around the anus. In the negative Oedipus complex of the genital stage passive femininity is expressed in the boy's wish to take the female role in copulation with the father. In Freud's view these biologically determined active-masculine and passive-feminine themes co-exist in all men.

Gender differentation theory proposes that the co-existence in the man of these patterns of masculinity and femininity is neither inevitable nor normal. It is rooted in development and signals disturbance in gender differentiation. It is linked to disturbance in the anal phase, specifically to the predominance of passivity over activity.

In Freud's sense, normally the two year old boy is active. In differentiation from his mother he becomes increasingly focussed on possession and autonomy. In identification with her in her child-bearing function he elaborates notions of his creative and productive capacities. He views these on the model of the digestive processes, and understands the production of babies in terms of the production of feces. The production of feces itself becomes a focus for issues of personal autonomy and possession as he learns to control his bowel movements. Significant passivity in the anal stage, the feeling of being the object of someone's action rather than the actor, suggests failure in the boy's accomplishment of phase-appropriate separation-individuation from the mother.

In optimum development gender differentiation occurs in the context of the secure establishment of 'activity' in the boy, his interest in mastery and autonomy. The attributes the boy characterizes as female as well as those he defines as male are founded on these earlier developments. The child-bearing capacities he perceives to be the prerogative of women have meanings for him of creativity and productivity in identification with his mother, and of autonomy and mastery as he sees them in terms of his own increasing bodily control. In successful gender differentiation he perceives both the woman and the man as centers of individual autonomy. Both men and women are experienced by the boy as active in Freud's sense of the word.

It is otherwise for the boy who has not successfully resolved the issues of differentiation from his mother, and is predominantly passive in the anal stage. The autonomous sense of self appropriate to the two year old is incompletely developed. Problems of separation and individuation from the mother persist. Rather than a confident interest in mastering his environment he has a continuing sense of being "done to," being the object of the other's action.

Recognition of sex difference brings new difficulties. Now he must perceive himself not only as an individual distinct from his mother but as being male distinct from his female mother. These new dimensions of difference between him and her may re-evoke unsolved separation issues. Not only is the mother a separate person independent of himself but in absolute ways her body differs from his own. Hers has characteristics absent in his. The very body parts that confirm his male identity are ones she does not have. The femininity he attributes to her he must renounce for himself.

If, in the context of incomplete self-other differentiation the boy does not successfully resolve issues of gender differentiation he may elaborate within himself a femininity that bears the stamp of the earlier bond to the mother (passivity) and of the incomplete gender differentiation (femininity). Its link with anal themes may be multiply determined in the relations of anality to both autonomy and femininity issues (in notions of anal birth). The man (or boy) in whom such a passive femininity persists may perceive with some accuracy that it represents the infantile or immature in himself, an incomplete development of autonomy and mastery, tendencies toward over-dependence on the mother, and a lack of masculinity (a castrated state). His attitude toward it may be one of contempt and repudiation. Freud views this pattern of femininity and of male reactions to femininity to be a biologically constituted, inevitable patterning as it is found in women as well as in men. Gender differentiation theory suggests it to be a pattern of femininity found in men who have not successfully resolved issues of gender differentiation.

Masculinity and Femininity: Sadism and Masochism

In Freud's view sexual sadism and masochism are also aspects of a biologically based masculinity and femininity. They are rooted in the activity and passivity of the anal phase and can properly be called sadism and masochism only when they are sexualized at entry into the genital phase. Sexual sadism has the biologically male function of overcoming the sexual resistance of the female. Masochism represents femaleness, the wish to take the passive role in copulation with a man and child-bearing. Their clearest clinical expression is in perversion.

As in the case of activity and passivity, gender differentiation theory suggests that sexual sadism and masochism do not represent biologically patterned masculinity and femininity as they regularly occur in men and in women. They represent aspects of a disturbed organization of masculinity and femininity in men, To anticipate, the man continues to elaborate both masculinity and femininity within himself. His sadism reflects his wish to humiliate the woman. His masochism is a defensive reversal of that wish in which he takes the role of the humiliated woman. The wish to humiliate appears to be related to an early stage in gender differentiation when the boy becomes aware of limits to his sex and gender possibilities. It appears to represent the boy's envious hatred against the mother who has what he lacks.

Evidence in support of these hypotheses is both theoretically and clinically based. Sexual sadism and masochism are not regularly found in men and in women, respectively. Both are generally recognized to be disorders of men. Their clearest clinical expression occurs in perversions, themselves almost exclusively disorders of males. Even Freud's discussion of "feminine masochism" (1924) concerns masochistic perversions in men. Moreover, sadism and masochism tend to occur as two faces of the same coin. When one occurs it is invariably accompanied by the other. Sadism is believed to be primary, masochism a defensive reversal of the sadistic aim (Freud, 1915).

The link of sadism-masochism to issues of sex difference is suggested theoretically by Freud's conception of its origin in the transition from the anal to the genital period, a transition marked by the recognition of sex difference. It is suggested as well by the observation that sadism-masochism regularly occurs in all forms of perverse development, itself a sex difference related disorder (Gillespie, 1952; Greenacre, 1953; Khan, 1965; Bak, 1968). The focus of the underlying issues is the mother. This is most evident in the fact that the overt expression of sexual sadism occurs in relation to the woman. However, it appears as well that a typical forerunner of sadism-masochism is the man's significant disturbance in separation from the mother. Such antecedents have been observed generally in perversions in which sadism-masochism regularly occurs (Socarides, 1960; Bak, 1968; Greenacre, 1968). They have been observed as well in cases specifically of masochism (Fenichel, 1928; Bychowski, 1959; Modell, 1965). Their relation to sadism has not been specified.

The aims of sadism-masochism and their underlying fantasies have been only partially explored. It is generally accepted that sadism is not, as Freud suggested, a normal expression of wooing, perhaps carried to excess. Its aim is to humiliate and to give pain. The fantasies impelling such aims are not explicated in the literature. They may be tentatively inferred from the defensive reversal of sadism in masochism. In masochistic acts the man is to be humiliated and given pain by a woman. The related fantasies concern pregnancy and childbirth (Freud, 1924). Freud interprets these wishes as an expression of biologically based femininity. If masochism is seen instead as the defensive reversal of sadism, another interpretation is possible. The original sadistic impulse, then, can be seen as a wish to humiliate the woman and give her pain. The context is her capacity for pregnancy and childbirth.

The gender differentiation perspective suggests that this wish is to humiliate the woman as the man has been humiliated by his recognition of sex difference. The unlimited potential he assumed for himself has proved illusory. Among the limits he must accept are ones involving child-bearing. The mother has the capacities he lacks. His envious hatred focuses on her. In his egocentric cognitive mode he equates the fact that she has what he wants with the idea that therefore she is the cause of his deprivation. The sadistic wish to humiliate the woman in connection with issues of pregnancy and childbirth may, if this line of reasoning proves valid, represent the boy's angry protest against the sex and gender limits he must accept when he becomes aware of sex difference.

Masculinity and Femininity: Some Differentiation Perspectives

Gender differentiation theory suggests that in optimum negotiation of the issues of sex difference the boy achieves a differentiated sense of masculinity and of femininity. His sense of himself as masculine is centered in his male body. He recognizes in persons of the other sex a femininity centered in their female bodies and functions. He views both masculinity and femininity to be valid and independent organizations. He elaborates the interplay of masculinity and femininity in object relations rather than within himself.

Biological factors contribute little to what is to be included in the boy's categories of masculinity and of femininity. Physiological factors may have some effect, but the available evidence indicates that generally in humans social factors override the physiological ones (Stoller, 1968). Freud emphasizes the physiological consequences of the anatomical and functional distinctions between the sexes. However, Mead (1967) points out on the basis of her intensive study of seven primitive cultures that the psychological consequences of the anatomical distinction between the sexes are by no means uniform among cultures. It is the social meaning of the anatomical differences that is determinitive, not the differences themselves. For instance, clinical observation suggests that in this society pregnancy is a major female function from which men and boys feel themselves to be excluded. However, the *meaning* of male envy of pregnancy is worth further study. As Ross (1977) points out it is unlikely that the boy is envious of the mother's capacity for actual gestation. That has little meaning in his own experience. It is possible that the notion of pregnancy functions as a symbol for the maternal capacities to nurture and comfort of which he has profound and intimate experience. From these the boy is by no means excluded on constitutional grounds.

The array of self representations available for categorization determine the initial content of the boy's categories of masculinity and femininity. These are established prior to the boy's awareness of sex difference in identification with parents and in the context of general environmental encouragement of masculinity. They are not masculine and feminine identifications that automatically define the eventual meanings of masculinity and femininity for him. It is not necessary therefore for the boy to dis-identify with the mother (Greenson, 1968) or to repudiate his identifications with her (Kestenberg, 1956). A broad range of identifications with her, including her functions in nurturing and caregiving may be included in his sense of himself as masculine. It may in fact be that "dis-identification" or "repudiation" signals failure in optimum development of masculinity, an organization too exclusively phallic, denying the actual procreative capacity and nurturing possibilities of the man.

In the differentiation process the categories of masculinity and femininity are elaborated reciprocally. Differentiation failure affects both. If the boy does not adequately apprehend the character of the female body his sense of the construction of the male body also remains insecure. If he believes all bodies to be alike and the girl a castrate because lacking a penis, he is likely to retain belief in anal birth and the consequent possibility that both men and women can bear children.

The man's notions of the relations between men and women may be colored by the internal relationships of his categories of masculinity and femininity. The man or boy who dreads his own feminine wishes may find association with actual women threatening. One who attempts to check an unrelinquished femininity in himself by scorn and derogation may also feel contempt for a woman however, without being able to relinquish his attachment to her. The man who perceives his own retained femininity as infantile, indicative of passivity, or incomplete masculinity may see these as actual characteristics of women.

Beyond issues of sex difference itself, differentiation processes in the oedipal period have major influences in patterning the boy's categories of masculinity and femininity. Although they are not the topic of this discussion, some indications of their character may anticipate directions for later discussion. It may be that the major gender differentiation processes of the oedipal period involve the boy testing the reality of the myriad notions of masculinity and femininity derived from pre-oedipal identifications and differentiation processes, and integrating them into relatively coherent wholes. The central figures for this reality testing are the parents, now newly perceived as masculine and feminine. In relation to his mother the boy must test and integrate his competing notions of femininity as all powerful, infantile, threatening, dependent, and so forth. He must differentiate from among his identifications with his mother those maternal identifications incompatible with his masculinity from those that are included in his mother's femininity but that may also be integral to his masculinity.

His father provides a model for what the boy may include in his notions of masculinity. In relation to him the boy tests and integrates his disparate notions of masculinity as all powerful, utterly lacking, masterful, exclusively phallic, and so on. Similarly, he forms his notions of appropriate relations of male to female, whether of mutual respect, derogation, envy, or wary defensiveness. As the father shares characteristics with the mother the boy learns how particular attributes may occur in the contexts of masculinity and of femininity. As the father teaches the boy and facilitates his development the boy is encouraged to integrate into his masculine identity notions originally developed in identification with his mother that lay the groundwork for fatherhood and more broadly generative interests, as Ross suggests (1977). In the Oedipus complex itself the boy may reach the epitome of phase-appropriate gender development. There, in competition and rivalry with the father for the mother, he works out not only the complexities of his newly patterned relationships to each parent, but the permutations of simultaneous investment in both.

SUMMARY

Gender development in boys is explored as a process of differentiation. An early period is posited in which boys' self-representations embodying their ideas of their sex and gender possibilities are not yet gender-differentiated. Differentiation processes begin when boys become aware of sex difference. That awareness entails the boy's recognition of the limits posed by his actual sex, a recategorization of his experience in gender terms, his elaboration of a masculine identity centered in his bodily maleness, his relinquishing of the female/feminine as possibilities for himself, and the recognition that they are the prerogatives of other-sex persons. Issues of bisexuality, castration anxiety, notions of "the phallic mother," and the equation of masculine-feminine with active-passive and sadistic-masochistic are examined from the perspective of differentiation theory in comparison with and contrast to Freud's theories of bisexuality and of male gender development.

REFERENCES

Bak, R. C. (1968). The phallic woman: The ubiquitous fantasy in perversions, *Psychoanal. Study Child,* 23: 15–36.

Bell, A. (1964). Bowel training difficulties in boys. *Amer. Acad. Child Psychiat.,* 3: 577–590.

Block, J. H. (1977). Another look at sex differentiation in the socialization behaviors of mothers and fathers. In J. Sherman and F. Denmark (eds.), *Psychology of Women: Future of Research,* New York: Psychological Dimensions.

Boehm, F. (1930). The femininity-complex in men. *Int. J. Psychoanal.,* 2: 444–469.

Buttenheim, M. (1979). Toward a psychoanalytic theory of rape. (Unpublished paper)

Bychowski, G. (1959). Some aspects of masochistic involvement. *Amer. Psychoanal. Assoc. J.,* 7: 248–273.

Fenichel, O. (1928). The clinical aspect of the need for punishment. *Int. J, Pyschoanal.,* 9: 47–70.

Freud, S. (1896). Extracts from the Fliess papers. *Standard Edition,* 1.

Freud, S. (1900). The interpretation of dreams. *Standard Edition,* 5.

Freud, S. (1908). Hysterical phantasies and their relation to bisexuality. *Standard Edition,* 9.

Freud, S. (1909a). Analysis of a phobia in a five-year-old boy. *Standard Edition,* 10.

Freud, S. (1909b). Notes upon a case of obsessional neurosis. *Standard Edition,* 10.

Freud, S. (1915). Instincts and their vicissitudes. *Standard Edition,* 14.

Freud, S. (1918). From the history of an infantile neurosis. *Standard Edition,* 17.

Freud, S. (1923). The infantile genital organization. *Standard Edition,* 19.

Freud, S. (1924). The economic problem of masochism. *Standard Edition,* 19.

Freud, S. (1927). Fetishism. *Standard Edition,* 21.

Freud, S. (1940). An outline of psychoanalysis. *Standard Edition,* 23.

Gillespie, W. H. (1952). Notes on the analysis of sexual perversions. *Int. J. Psychoanal.,* 33: 397–402.

Greenacre, P. (1953). Certain relationships between fetishism and faulty development of the body image. *Psychoanal. Study Child,* 8: 79–98.

Greenacre, P. (1968). Perversions: general considerations regarding their genetic and dynamic background, *Psychoanal. Study Child,* 23: 47–62.

Greenson, R. R. (1968). Dis-identifying with the mother; Its special importance for the boy. *Int. J. Psychoanal.,* 49: 370–373.

Jacobson, E. (1950). Development of the wish for a child in boys. *Psychoanal, Study Child,* 5: 139–152.

Kestenberg, J. (1956). On the development of maternal feelings in early childhood. *Psychoanal. Study Child,* 11: 257–291.

Khan, M. (1965). Foreskin fetishism and its relation to ego pathology. *Int. J. Psychoanal.,* 46: 64–80.

Kleeman, J. A. (1966). Genital self-discovery during a boy's second year. *Psychoanal. Study Child,* 21: 358–392.

Lorand, S. (1939). The role of the female penis fantasy in male character formation. *Int J. Psychoanal.,* 20: 171–182.

Mead, M. (1967). *Male and female.* New York: Wm Morrow and Company.

Modell, A. H. (1965). On having the right to a life: An aspect of the superego's development. *Int. J. Psychoanal.,* 46: 323–331.

Ross, J. M. (1977). Towards Fatherhood: The epigenesis of paternal identity during a boy's first decade. *Int. Rev. Psychoanal.,* 4: 327–347.

Socarides, C. W. (1960). The development of a fetishistic perversion. *J. Amer. Psychoanal. Assoc.,* 8: 281–311.

Sperling, M. (1964). The analysis of a boy with transvestite tendencies. *Psychoanal. Study Child.* 19: 470–493.

Stoller, R. J. (1968). *Sex and Gender.* New York: Jason Aronson.

4 Gender Differentiation and the Oedipus Complex

INTRODUCTION

Children's developments in gender identity and in same-sex and cross-sex relations following their recognition of sex difference are major foci of interest in Freud's formulations of the Oedipus complex. In gender differentiation terms these developments concern the establishment of subjective definitions of masculinity and femininity, gender appropriate self-definition (both bodily and social), and the definition in gender terms of same-sex and cross-sex relationships.

Subjective definitions of masculinity and femininity must be distinguished from objective ones. Objectively defined, individuals' characteristics are masculine or feminine to the extent that they are typical of one or the other sex in a particular social group. Subjective definitions refer to personal constructs of masculinity and femininity, individuals' own notions, applied to themselves and to others, of what it is to be masculine and feminine.

To make that distinction suggests various possible relations between the two. The most common one, fostered by the individual's social environment, is a match between them. It can happen, however, that a trait objectively defined as masculine or feminine is not so defined subjectively. The daughter of a professional woman, for example, may include career ambitions in her personal construct of femininity though her social group does not. It may be that a characteristic not defined as gender specific by the society is so defined by the individual, as occurs when a man categorizes all creativity and productivity as feminine and therefore alien to himself as masculine. Objectively sex-specific behavior may occur without subjective gender definition. That is regularly true of children before awareness of sex difference.

The distinction between subjective and objective definition of masculinity and femininity is not consistently made in either the academic-empirical or the psychoanalytic-clinical literature. In the empirical literature the focus has been almost exclusively on objective definition, for example, on the extent to which individual's observed characteristics or self-ratings correspond to those typical of one sex or the other, or on influences on the development of gender-appropriate behavior. The pervading assumption, usually implicit, is that subjective definitions match the objective ones. The possibility of discrepancy between them or the implications of such discrepancy have not been of investigative interest, for example, the degree to which men might include in their self-definition *as masculine,* sensitivity to and care for the needs of their children and their work associates, or differences in the patterning of nurturant behavior in men between those for whom it is integral to their masculine self-definitions and those for whom it is a reflection of "maternal" orientations they "also" have.

In Freud's thinking the focus is centrally on subjective definition, individuals' personal experience of masculinity and femininity. However, in his thinking too, objective and subjective definition tends to be fused. Freud's assumption in both his bisexuality theory and his developmental theory is that the characteristics of masculinity and femininity are biologically determined, activity and sadism are inherently masculine, passivity and masochism feminine. They are experienced as such by individuals (i.e., as subjectively defined), and observation of active orientations in an individual (male or female) can safely be inferred to represent masculine trends, passivity to represent feminine ones.

In neither the academic nor the clinical literature has the *development* of subjective definitions of masculinity and femininity been a significant focus of investigation. Maccoby and Jacklin (1974), for example, list only a few relevant studies. They concern children's acquisition by about age four, of fairly stable concepts of their own sexual identities as boy or girl that include recognition that these imply certain adult functions (being a father or a mother) not subject to change.

In Freud's thinking the complexities of masculine and feminine development are of central interest, but the interest is not in the development of masculinity and femininity per se. That development is seen to be biologically determined. Investigative interest has been in the complexities of the *interplay* of masculinity and femininity in the personality, and in patterns of *interference* with the normal (biologically determined) developmental progression toward the activity and sadism of masculinity, and the passivity and masochism of femininity.

Exploration of the interplay of masculinity and femininity occurs largely in the context of bisexuality theory. In that theory the characteristics of masculinity and femininity are explicitly biological givens and their formation is not itself of investigative concern. Developmental interest is focused on their interplay, for instance in the phenomena of the negative Oedipus complex or in their contribution to boys' castration anxiety on recognition of sex difference.

Patterns of interference with normal development have been explored more intensively in the context of Freud's developmental theory. However, the premises of this theory too, dictate that masculine activity and sadism, and feminine passivity and masochism are universal maturational products. Investigation is directed toward conflict-based interferences with developmental progressions toward these normal outcomes. Questions do not arise about boys' *learning* to perceive their genital excitements as masculine, *learning* to integrate these with their burgeoning notions of what it is to be a boy, or *learning* to include in their sense of themselves as masculine, tendencies toward activity and sadism. Similarly, investigations of gender development in girls do not focus on girls' *learning* to identify clitoral experiences as masculine, or *learning* to perceive active mastery as unfeminine. Their learning of passivity and masochism is considered to be inevitable and normal, consequent on the biological facts of their (and males') anatomical structure.

The focus of this chapter is the delineation of an alternate framework for understanding the development of subjective definitions of masculinity and femininity. It suggests that individuals' personal gender constructs are established, in and structured by the processes of gender differentiation. It proposes that major developments in the establishment of personal gender constructs begin when children become focally aware of sex difference and continue through what is generally referred to as the oedipal period. Moreover, it hypothesizes that to a significant degree Freud's observations of the phenomena attendant on recognition of sex difference and of the oedipal period can usefully be understood as gender differentiation phenomena integral to children's establishment of subjective gender constructs, self identification in terms of those constructs and the elaboration of same-sex and cross-sex relations to parents newly seen in terms of their masculinity and femininity.

The major observations on which Freud based his theory of the Oedipus complex are that at about two or three years of age children become focally interested in their genitals and in the differences between the sexes. They begin to identify genital differences with gender differences. Their recognition of sex difference is regularly associated with anxiety about genital loss or damage. It initiates the elaboration of the same-sex and cross-sex relationships and identifications which comprise the Oedipus complex.

In his conceptual formulation of these observations Freud hypothesized that this interest of children in their genitals represents children's first focal genital interest. It is stimulated by a biologically based intensification of genital sensation. This genital experience is male (penile and clitoral) and masculine in aim (active and sadistic). Interest in sex difference follows naturally. The associated anxiety in both boys and girls concerns loss of or damage to the penis. The phenomena of the Oedipus complex follow, also biologically determined, though not in ways that are clearly specified.

The differentiation paradigm offers an alternate interpretation of these observations. Children's new and complex involvements with their genitals in sex difference terms, and with their parents in terms of same-sex and cross-sex relationships (oedipal phenomena) are viewed as reflecting two aspects of the gender differentiation processes, one a bodily focus, the other a social one.

Children's intensification of interest in their genitals is not ascribed to unknown biological processes but to the beginning of a complex redefinition of their genital experience in gender terms. Genital experience is not hypothesized to become focal for the first time now. Rather, current evidence suggests that children have typically established an extensive body of genital experience prior to this time. That experience, however, is not subjectively male (or female) from its beginnings. It begins to become so when gender concepts become relevant for children. The intensification of genital interest specifically concerns newly developing perceptions of the genitals in gender terms and the complex anxieties and reorientations that accompany it.

The social developments in which same-sex and cross-sex relationships are elaborated are not ascribed to an Oedipus complex that springs *sui generis* from a biological matrix and imposes itself on children's relationships to their parents. They reflect the complexities that occur when children restructure their relations to their parents in the context of a newly differentiated sex-specific personal identity in relation to a mother newly perceived as female and a father as male. It is in the complexities of these gender differentiation processes related to their bodies and to their interpersonal relationships that children forge their personal constructs of masculinity and femininity.

GENDER-RELEVANT BODILY AND SOCIAL
EXPERIENCE PRIOR TO GENDER
DIFFERENTIATON

There is growing evidence that, prior to the intensification of genital involvement that accompanies interest in sex difference and initiates the oedipal period, children have established an extensive base of gender-relevant bodily (genital) and social experience. Before they become focally interested in sex difference children are likely to have extensive experience of sex-specific aspects of the adult and child bodies of others of both sexes. From birth they have experience of the genital areas of their bodies arising from anatomic structure and whatever sex-specific physiological processes may be operative. They have interpersonal experience of their genital areas in the context of child care. As they explore their bodies they achieve increasingly articulated knowledge of their genitals. Well before interest in sex difference, probably at about 18 months of age, they typically become interested in satisfying self-stimulation of their genitals (Kleeman, 1966; Galenson & Roiphe, 1977; Parens, Pollock, Stern, & Krama, 1977). The bodily differences between their mothers and fathers become familiar in the intimacies of daily experience. Contacts with same-sex and other-sex children typically provide further experience of bodily differences. There is no basis, however, for the notion that these experiences, objectively sex-specific, are differentially categorized by infants as masculine and feminine.

Significant gender relevant social experiences also occur before the beginnings of gender differentiation. As Stoller (1968) points out, these begin with sex-ascription at birth. From that time the caretaking environment treats boys and girls in ways that encourage the development of gender appropriate characteristics (Mead, 1967; Stoller, 1968; Block, 1973). From the beginning children are establishing identifications with their parents and patterns of both same-sex and cross-sex relationships to them. Mothers, female themselves, encourage boys' masculine development, as well as identification, and boys simultaneously have experience of same-sex relations and identifications with their fathers. Girls, conversely, establish same-sex and identificatory relationships with their mothers and are encouraged in their feminine development as well, by their fathers, in relation to the fathers' own masculinity.

Conceptual bases for gender differentiation are also laid. Before children become aware of sex difference they know the terms "boy" and "girl." They identify themselves accurately and have begun to define father and mother, children, animals, and toys in those terms.

These developments lay the foundation for gender differentiation. Children's experiences of their genitals are objectively male or female. Their experiences of their mothers' and fathers' bodies are objectively of females and males. Behaviors encouraged by the caretaking environment are those the society finds appropriate to children's actual sex. Objectively same-sex and cross-sex relationships and identifications are established between children and their parents. In the proposed view, however, children have not *subjectively* differentiated these experiences in gender terms. They do not yet have subjective definitions of masculinity and femininity.

THE RECONCEPTUALIZATION OF GENITAL EXPERIENCE IN GENDER TERMS

Gender differentiation theory suggests that the observed intensification of children's genital interests when they become aware of sex difference is consequent on a new *focus* of interest, the recategorization in gender terms of an already well-established body of genital experience. It suggests that children's accurate definition of their genitals as male or female is not determined by their very structure and associated physiological processes, but is learned. This learning is gradual, beginning with a relatively diffuse and undifferentiated sense that the characteristics of one's "bottom" are related to oneself as "boy" or "girl," and culminating in an accurate perception of one's genitals (and those of other persons) and a recognition that they are sex-specific.

It seems likely that in the first stages of their awareness that their genitals are involved in gender definition, children identify their genital experience as part of themselves as girl or as boy. Their sense of the relevant body parts is likely to be general, including excretory organs and functions as well as genital ones. Although children may already have identified these body organs denotatively in gender terms, their subjective definitions of them are not yet made in sex difference terms.

The implications of this proposition are different than those proceeding from Freud's formulation. They suggest that the girl's first gender-specific experience of her genitals is not as male, but is identified with herself as "girl." For both boys and girls the body parts involved are not limited to penis and clitoris but probably include genital and excretory organs in relatively non-specific ways. The associated experience is not of a biologically patterned maleness but is what the child includes in his or her sense of being a boy or a girl. This sense of self as "boy" or "girl" is not elaborated in sex difference terms, and not yet limited to the realities of actual maleness and femaleness.

They suggest, moreover, that in some cases individuals may fail to establish a focal and accurate sense of their genitals as sex-specific and the bodily center of their masculine or feminine identities. Such failures have been commonly observed in girls and women. Greenacre's (1953) and Socarides' (1960) observations of what appear to be such failures in men are discussed in Chapter 3.

Freud's model allows for such failures in women but not in men. In his view, men's sense of maleness, centered in the penis, is biologically determined and inevitable; children's penile and clitoral sensations that initiate the oedipal period are male, and form an inevitable and indissoluble bond between male anatomy and subjective experience of maleness. Women, however, have no sense of genital femaleness in childhood, and, moreover, have a sense of genital (clitoral) maleness that must be repudiated. A re-focus of genital interest onto the vagina must occur in adolescence or adulthood if they are to arrive at a sense of themselves as female which is centered in their female bodies. Failure in this complicated sequence is not unlikely.

The differentiation paradigm proposes further, that children differentiate their subjective definitions of bodily maleness and femaleness out of their more general ideas of body areas relevant to their identities as "boy" or "girl." It suggests that for both boys and girls this process begins with a recognition of bodily limit. A temporary sense of one's own body as utterly lacking anything worthwhile may alternate with a sense of other-sex bodies as lacking or damaged. In girls the sense of lack tends to focus on the penis, in boys on the capacity to bear children.

In this too, the proposed perspective differs from Freud's. In his view boys do not become aware of a bodily limit. The capacity to bear children is not an issue of sex difference for them. It is inevitable (and normal) for boys to perceive girls as utterly lacking (castrated) and this perception does not alternate with a sense of their own bodies as incomplete or lacking something worthwhile. It is equally inevitable for girls to recognize their bodily limit. Its focus is the penis. This recognition does not alternate with a perception of themselves as complete and other-sex persons as lacking.

The proposed view provides a possible solution for a persistent problem in the psychoanalytic conceptualization of castration anxiety. Specifically, Freud auggested that when children become aware of sex difference they regularly experience an anxiety he called castration anxiety. It occurs identically in boys and girls. In both it concerns loss of the penis. Boys fear that they might be castrated as they perceive girls to be. Girls feel that, not having a penis, they have been castrated.

From the beginning this formulation has been the subject of heated criticism. The presence of genital anxiety in both boys and girls when they become aware of sex difference has not been successfully challenged. The focus of objections to Freud's formulation and attempts at a satisfactory reformulation have focused on the notion that girls feel a sense of loss at not having male genitals. Abraham (1920) considered the possibility of a more general genital anxiety in girls that would

include girls' anxiety about their own genitals, but his observations convinced him that girls' anxiety did indeed concern
loss of maleness. Rado (1933) thoroughly criticized the notion
that a girl's anxiety over the loss of a penis she never had
could be like that of the boy over the loss of an actual body
part. He suggested that the formulation concerning girls was
in error, but he did not offer a generally accepted alternative.
Jacobson (1976) considered the widely accepted argument
that girls' anxieties concerned a sense of accomplished loss
and boys' an impending one but found no support for such a
difference in her clinical data. The consensus remained that
girls do indeed suffer anxieties over the loss of maleness, and
that therefore boys' and girls' castration anxieties are identical, but that no thoroughly acceptable explanation was
available.

The differentiation perspective suggests that the search for
a solution was misdirected. It suggests that before gender
differentiation children's ideas of their genital attributes and
potentials are not limited by their actual sex. The differentiation process begins with a recognition of limits, girls' recognition that what is exclusively male is outside their prerogative,
boys' that the possibilities of female genital capacities are
absolutely closed to them. Children feel these limits as losses.
It is this sense of loss that is represented in the "castration"
anxiety attendant on recognition of sex difference. It does occur in both boys and girls. In both it is an illusory loss. Girls'
anxiety does indeed concern the lack of maleness. It is boys'
anxiety that has been misconstrued. Boys' later castration
anxiety, stemming from the rivalrous relation to the father
does centrally concern the loss of genital maleness. However,
their earlier genital anxiety, attendant on recognition of sex
difference is hypothesized in differentiation theory, to concern
centrally the lack of female capacities. Evidence for this view
is presented in Chapter 3. That is, the observed castration
anxiety found to be identical in boys and girls refers to that
attendant on recognition of sex difference. It is identical in
being responsive to recognition of limits. Its content is different. Girls' anxieties do concern loss of maleness. Boys,' however, concern loss of femaleness. It is boys' later rivalry-based

anxiety in relation to their fathers that centrally concerns loss of the penis.

Following the initial recognition of limits, in the process of differentiation proper, children are hypothesized to differentiate their subjective notions of bodily maleness and femaleness in complement to one another. There are indications that in the initial stages of this differentiation children elaborate both maleness and femaleness in the context of their own bodies. Only gradually, it appears, is this narcissistic elaboration replaced by an interpersonal one in which the child's own genitals, appropriately defined in gender terms, are integrated as part of self, and other-sex genital organization, accurately perceived, is attributed to persons of the other sex.

Clinical observation suggests that the possibilities for elaborating a sense of male and female within one's own body are virtually limitless (feces in anus, finger in nose, penis in hand, piercing sound in ear, tongue in mouth, etc.). Developmentally most common, however, appears to be boys' identification of penis as male and anus as female, and girls' perception of vagina (and internal accompaniments) as female and clitoris as male.

This hypothesis places Freud's observation of girls' and womens' identification of the clitoris as male, and subsequent confirming clinical observation, in a new context. It does not suggest that the clitoris is biologically male or that the girl's first genital experience is male. It suggests, rather, that the girl's identification of clitoral experience with maleness is a developmental accomplishment and phase appropriate at a particular stage in the gender differentiation process. It does not occur as the girl's sole genital experience but in complement to notions of femaleness she is also developing. In optimal development it is replaced by an interpersonal elaboration of constructs of genital sex differences in which the girl accurately attributes maleness to the genitals of boys and men in relation to her own female genitals. Clitoral experience is included with the rest of her genital apparatus as the bodily center of her female experience. The later retention of notions of clitoral experience as male represents incomplete gender differentitaion, failure to complete the transition from a narcissistic elaboration of maleness and femaleness within one's own body, to an interpersonal elaboration of one's own bodily self as female in relation to the male bodies of other-sex persons.

The boy, similarly, is hypothesized initially to differentiate notions of both maleness and femaleness within his own body. Out of the generalized sense of self as "boy" he typically differentiates temporary notions of maleness centered in his penis and of femaleness centered in the anal area. In optimum development he, like the girl, replaces these notions with an interpersonal elaboration of his subjective definitions of the genitals. Female genitals, now accurately perceived, are attributed to women and perceived to be complementary to his own male genitals. When gender differentiation remains incomplete or is disturbed the boy may retain notions of his genitals in which the penis is male and the anus female. If anal organs and functions continue to be perceived as female aspects of himself his sense of himself as genitally male remains insecure, and his masculine identity cannot be unequivocally centered in bodily maleness.

To summarize, gender differentiation theory proposes a formulation in major ways the reverse of Freud's. In Freud's view the genitals and their associated aims are objectively sex-specific, and they determine subjective definitions of maleness and femaleness. Gender differentiation theory suggests that genital experience is objectively sex-specific, but subjective definition of genital organs and experience as male and female is learned. It suggests that before differentiation processes begin children's genital experience is well-established but children do not categorize it in gender terms, nor recognize limits imposed by their actual sex. When they first become aware that their genitals are involved in gender definition they identify the genital and excretory areas generally with themselves as "boy" or "girl." More focal recognition of sex-difference and gender differentiation processes begin with the awareness of genital limit and attendant anxiety focused on perceived genital loss. In the course of differentiation processes a temporary phase-specific period is hypothesized to occur in which children identify both bodily maleness and femaleness in their own bodies. This is gradually replaced by interpersonal elaboration in which one's own genitals and those of the other sex are accurately perceived and subjectively defined as both sex-specific and related to one another. In sum, in Freud's view personal gender constructs are the psychical consequences of the anatomical distinction between the sexes. In the view of gender differentiation theory, subjective definition of the genitals as male and female is structured by the psychical processes involved in gender differentiation.

THE REDEFINITION OF SOCIAL EXPERIENCE IN GENDER TERMS

The differentiation theory proposal that genital experience, which is objectively male or female, becomes subjectively defined in gender terms by children in the course of gender differentiation processes, has implications for conceptualizing gender-related changes in children's interpersonal relations. In Freud's view, the changes in interpersonal relations are the direct result of genital experience or bisexual tendencies that are both objectively male or female and subjectively experienced as such. In boys (developmental theory) male genital experience initiates the Oedipus complex. It leads to rivalry with the father for possession of the mother, castration anxiety that expresses the boy's fear of retaliation from the father, and identification with the father and his values. Boys' relations to their mothers, having been heterosexual since birth, do not change. A feminine orientation in boys that precedes the Oedipus complex is also rooted in biological processes. It is the expression of the feminine theme of an innate bisexuality (bisexuality theory).

In girls, the development of a feminine identity and gender appropriate interpersonal relations is reactive to their earlier (clitoral) masculinity. When they become aware of sex difference, girls recognize themselves to be castrated. They give up clitoral masturbation with its masculine active-sadistic aims and move toward passivity and masochism. They repudiate their mothers as cause of their castration. They turn to their fathers, first to get a penis from him, then, in a feminine orientation, a baby.

That is, Freud's observations led him to the recognition, now widely accepted, that children in their third and fourth years of life acquire subjective definitions of masculinity and femininity, establish their own gender identities, and develop patterns of same-sex and cross-sex relations in the context of their relationships to their mothers and fathers. He conceptualized these developments as parameters of the positive and the negative Oedipus complex. In his view, these developments were direct consequences of biological processes.

Differentiation theory proposes that experience which is objectively male or female is not automatically so defined subjectively by children. The gender definition of genital experience is itself a developmental accomplishment. Therefore, genital experience per se cannot constitute or produce children's subjective definitions of social masculinity and femininity, and their sense of themselves as masculine or feminine. Nor can it set in train the processes by which enduring same-sex and cross-sex relationship patterns are established. Differentiation theory suggests instead that subjective gender definitions, a personal gender identity, and the formation of same-sex and cross-sex relations can be understood as developmental outcomes of differentiation processes.

Gender-inappropriate Orientations: A Feminine Phase in Boys, A Masculine (Phallic) One in Girls

Psychoanalytic thinking divides the oedipal period roughly into two stages. The first of these can be seen to include the negative Oedipus complex, the phallic stage in girls and a feminine phase in boys. The second deals more specifically with the Oedipus complex proper. These are by no means strictly consecutive stages, but the distinction is conceptually useful and will be used here as well.

Discussion of the first period focuses on the occurance of gender-inappropriate orientations in the personality, masculinity in girls and femininity in boys. Freud's observation, that bisexual orientations occur in adult men and women and that they originate in this developmental period is widely accepted. However, his conceptualization has significant problems. In his view bisexuality occurs in girls because their genitals themselves are bisexual. Their first sex and gender experience is exclusively male and masculine. Their feminine identity is superimposed on the masculine one and requires a shift from the early focus of genital sensation in the clitoris to the vagina. Therefore residues of masculinity or its regressive resurgence in neurosis are expectable in girls and women. Comparable difficulties are less likely to occur in boys and men because their development is straightforwardly masculine (developmental theory). This formulation is not supported by clinical observation. The expectation that women are less sure than men of their gender identities is not borne out. Men's fears that they are not truly masculine, or that their identity as male may be lost, appear to be more frequent than comparable fears in women. In regression, feelings that one is becoming the other sex are not infrequent in men but they occur rarely in women. Homosexual object choice in adulthood, which Freud believed to be related to bisexuality, does not appear to occur more frequently in women than in men. Moreover, in severe disturbances of adolescence in which girls may fear lesbian relationships, the typical dynamic content appears to be the sexualization of wishes for fusion with the mother in a two-person unity rather than a wish for a heterosexual union with her in which the girl assumes a male role. The presence of male and female themes in men has no place in Freud's developmental theory. All biological and social factors predispose boys exclusively to masculinity. To account for bisexuality in men Freud proposed a biologically based universal bisexuality which is the cause of boys' wishes to assume a feminine role with their fathers. The incompatibility of this theory with the developmental theory has been discussed in Chapter 3. Its proposal that without reason in development or context in familial relationships a phase regularly occurs in boys in which they wish to take a female role with their fathers (to be sexually penetrated by the father and, perhaps, to have a baby by him) is unsatisfactory.

Gender differentiation theory suggests instead that bisexuality in both boys and girls is a developmental product. From sex ascription at birth children have been encouraged in directions that are objectively masculine or feminine. Their self representations (identifications), therefore, are likely to be preponderantly gender-appropriate. However, their self representations are not yet limited by recognition of their actual gender. When children become aware of sex difference they begin to recategorize their self representations (bodily and social) in gender terms. It seems likely that for a time, (probably when it is also true of male and female body parts), they elaborate their subjective definitions of masculinity and femininity within themselves. Gradually they recognize that only one gender organization is theirs, the one appropriate to their body structure (and, normally, the one socially most familiar and most extensively elaborated). The other is the prerogative of other-sex persons and can be enjoyed in relationship but not as part of one's self.

This perspective suggests that the existence of subjective definitions of masculinity and femininity is a developmental accomplishment not a biological given. Greenacre's (1968) and Socarides' (1960) discussions of cases of perversion suggest that in some men, at least, delineated subjective constructs of what it is to be male and what it is to be female have failed to develop (see Chapter 3). It suggests that what may be included in these subjective definitions is not biologically determined but depends on the body of self representations with which children enter the differentiation process and on their continuing experience. Stoller (1968), for example, in his discussion of male transsexual development, shows some relations between major environmental failure in the early encouragement of gender-appropriate development and subsequent difficulty in boys' subjective definition of themselves as masculine. It suggests that bisexuality is established in boys and girls by similar processes, and that the masculine and feminine components are developed concurrently, not as in Freud's view of girls' development, one superimposed on the other. It suggests finally, that the continuing existence of bisexuality in adult-hood is not biologically ordained. It is a developmental in-completeness in the move from a narcissistic to an object-related elaboration of masculinity and femininity and signals disturbance in both the individual's gender identity and in his or her perception of and relation to other-sex persons.

This formulation also alters the perspective within which the "phallic" phase in girls and the now generally recognized feminine phase in boys (Boehm, 1930; Kestenberg, 1968; Greenson, 1968) can be understood. In current psychoanalytic thinking these are normal developmental phases that occur prior to children's definitive establishment of their gender-appropriate identities. The shift from the prior gender-inap-propriate orientation to the appropriate one is perceived to require that children repudiate or reject the former and estab-lish a sex-appropriate counter-identification. Conceptualiza-tion of these developments in girls has received little recent attention and there has been no generally accepted replace-ment of Freud's formulation of a phallic phase in girls based on male clitoral sensation, followed by the repudiation of mas-culine and homosexual orientations and succeeded in turn by a feminine orientation. More attention has been devoted to the reconceptualization of these phenomena in boys. There ap-pears to be a general consensus now that the feminine phase in boys cannot usefully be viewed as the expression toward the father of the feminine aspect of an inherent bisexuality, but must be seen as occurring in identification with the mother.

Significant conceptual difficulties remain, however. Similar developmental sequences from the gender-inappropriate phase, through its repudiation, to an ultimate gender-appro-priate identity are described as typical of boys and girls. How-ever, the hypothesized factors that result in the sequences differ in ways that are not easily resolved. On one hand Freud's explanation of the sequence in girls has no counterpart in his theory of boys' development, and it is not easy to imagine a satisfactory one. On the other hand, the explanation of the boy's feminine phase as an identification with the mother, his primary caretaker, cannot be symmetrically applied to the girls masculine phase because her primary caretaker is not a male but is also the mother. The developmental contexts for these sequences are also incompletely specified. Freud's hypothesis that the girl's phallic phase is specifically the product of male clitoral sensation and related masculine aim is untenable in light of current biological knowledge (see Chapters 1 and 2).

The notion that the boy's feminine phase occurs in identification with the mother raises other questions concerning the period out of which this feminine phase develops, the factors related to its onset and the parameters of the subsequent shift to masculinity. For example, if the boy's development prior to the feminine phase is thought to occur in a generally masculine direction, question arises as to reasons for the shift to a feminine orientation, the fate of the masculinity during the feminine phase and the relation of the prior masculinity to the masculinity that follows it. If, on the other hand, the early development in the boy is conceptualized as centrally feminine, based on identifications with the mother, question arises as to the different nature of the identifications with the mother that at a particular point constitute a feminine phase and about the bases in development for the subsequent gender-appropriate masculine identifications.

The differentiation paradigm suggests that the masculine phase in girls and the feminine one in boys are developmentally appropriate at a particular stage in the gender differentiation processes. Objectively, children's prior development has occurred in a predominantly gender appropriate way though without subjective recognition by children of the limits set by their actual gender. Gradually children begin to differentiate out of their own array of self-representations those appropriate to their own sex and those which are not. These form their initial subjective definitions of masculinity and femininity. Gradually they begin to attribute to other-sex persons the group of gender characteristics they have defined as appropriate to them, For a time the body of other-sex characteristics (masculinity for girls, femininity for boys) is likely to be highlighted as a center of conflict. The characteristics included in it have been included as self and are valued. To give them up is a narcissistic loss.

In this perspective the phallic phase in girls and the feminine phase in boys are seen as symmetrical developments. They follow a period in which children's self-representations include characteristics they will later assign to both masculinity and femininity, in a still undifferentiated array. Therefore, no new factor (e. g., a biological change in genital sensitivity or the emergence of innate bisexuality) needs to be postulated to account for the occurrence of gender-inappropriate orientations. For these to occur requires only that the previously undifferentiated array of self-representations be differentiated into two groups, one subjectively experienced as masculine, the other as feminine, one ego-syntonic and the other not.

The two are hypothesized to develop concurrently. For a time they may properly be seen as alternative identities (each carries the sense of "I," each is elaborated in self-other relationships, threat of loss of either may be experienced as a danger of identity loss). The observed phenomena of the girl's phallic phase and the boy's feminine one can be encompassed by this formulation. Freud's observations of girls' repudiation of their mothers and wanting a penis like their fathers' (and the relevant gender characteristics) may be understood as part of girls' growing recognition that what they have included in their constructs of masculinity cannot be theirs, and their assertive protest against this reality. The differentiation paradigm would argue, however, that simultaneously girls' subjective definitions of femininity are developing and are also felt as "I." Therefore, the repudiation of the mother is normally not complete, and with the wish to be like the father, a simultaneous cross-sex relationship to him is developing that typically becomes dominant as the girl increasingly attributes masculinity to other-sex persons and elaborates her own identity (apart from relatively conflict-free fantasy or dream) as exclusively feminine.

Boys' feminine orientations, in Freud's view (the negative Oedipus complex), are expressions of the feminine aspect of an innate universal bisexuality. In his view they came to the fore at this time because, on recognition of sex difference, boys realize that they must give up the possibility of realizing the feminine aspects of themselves (bisexuality theory). The differentiation perspective is similar in suggesting that the feminine aspects are part of the boy's self, and that they emerge in the context of the recognition that they must be given up as possibilities for himself. It also differs from Freud's. It suggests that this femininity has developmental rather than biological origins. The content of the femininity is a product of experience rather than of genetic definition. In normal development it does not persist through life as an ongoing theme balanced by concurrent masculinity. It is phase-appropriate at this early stage, but normally the narcissistic elaboration of masculinity and femininity is replaced by an unequivocal attribution of femininity to women and masculinity to self. Freud suggests further that the feminine theme in boys is expressed in wishes to be sexually penetrated by the father and to receive a child from him. (The latter wish is less frequently mentioned and is contrary to Freud's repeated insistence that boys' wishes to bear children are not feminine wishes and play no part in issues of sex difference.) Differentiation theory would suggest, instead, that boys (and girls) are likely to express, in relation to their parents, every aspect of same-sex and cross-sex relationships as they move toward a resolution of sex difference issues. These would include not only those that Freud mentions, but every aspect of masculinity and of femininity in relation to both father and mother.

More recent conceptualizations of boys' feminine phase as occurring in identification with their mothers can also be understood in a differentiation context and also can be given a more extensive framework. The differentiation model proposes that the characteristics expressed in the feminine phase are those the boy has included in his subjective definition of femininity. Many of these are likely to have been learned in identification with his mother. Of the great array of his identifications with his mother, however, only those that he has defined (rightly or wrongly) to be specific to femininity and not compatible with his masculinity will be expressed in the feminine phase. Differentiation theory suggests, moreover, that during this "feminine phase" the boy is concurrently elaborating his subjective definition of masculinity in complementary relation to his notions of femininity. It is, therefore, not altogether properly termed a feminine phase, being instead a phase in which masculinity and femininity are both being differentiated, but femininity, the focus of conflict, is highlighted.

Both in Freud's view and in more recent conceptions it appears that, at a given time, children repudiate the gender-inappropriate role and move on to the appropriate one. The boy, in Freud's view (bisexuality theory), does so in the context of a specific form of castration anxiety, the recognition that if he does not give up his feminine wishes he cannot be male. More recent formulations tend not to address the issue of what stimulates the boy's repudiation of the feminine phase. The girl, in Freud's view (developmental formulation), rejects clitoral masturbation (with its masculine aims) in disappointment at not having a penis and repudiates her mother (and her homosexual orientations) because she holds the mother responsible for her castration, thus giving up her masculine orientation and moving toward a feminine one. Following the repudiation of the gender-inappropriate phase, children are hypothesized to assume the gender appropriate one. The boy, in Freud's view (bisexuality theory), having given up the feminine position, actualizes the biologically determined aspect of his bisexuality. In more recent views he rejects his identifications with his mother, but the source of his subsequent masculinity is largely unspecified. The girl, in Freud's view (developmental theory), turns from her mother to her father, initially to get a penis from him, then to receive a baby, but the reason, in either biology or development, for the latter shift is unspecified other than by implication that this development is in line with biological destiny.

The gender differentiation paradigm suggests a different framework for these developments. It suggests that in normal development boys and girls do not repudiate or reject the femininity or masculinity that are inappropriate to their actual sex. Nor do they assume for themselves a hitherto unknown gender-appropriate orientation. In the course of the simultaneous differentiation of complementary subjective definitions of masculinity and femininity, each of which has the quality of an identity for a time, they gradually recognize the gender identity inappropriate to themselves as the prerogative of other-sex persons and unequivocally commit themselves to the gender-appropriate one. Gender differentiation theory suggests in fact, that the *repudiation* of the masculinity or femininity appropriate to the other-sex signals gender disturbance. It tends to reflect a failure to attribute other-sex gender identity unequivocally to other-sex persons. The repudiated gender, identity remains part of the self, unaccepted, but not given up. Under those circumstances the individual's gender-appropriate identity cannot be securely established. In other words, only as the other-sex gender identity is unequivocally perceived to be the prerogative of other-sex persons can individuals feel secure in their own gender-appropriate identities.

To summarize, it is generally accepted in psychoanalytic psychology that bisexual themes may be observed in men and women. Formulations of their origins have been stimulated by the observation of gender-inappropriate orientations in children in the period after they have become aware of sex difference but before the processes of the Oedipus complex become dominant. They include Freud's conceptualizations of a biologically based phallic period in girls and a negative Oedipus complex in boys, and in formulations emphasizing a feminine phase in boys rooted in identification with the mother. Gender differentiation theory proposes that these gender-inappropriate orientations occur when children have established in an elementary form, subjective constructs of masculinity and femininity. These are differentiated together, initially, as two complementary identity formations. The gender-inappropriate one is highlighted for a time because it becomes a focus of conflict when children become aware that they must give it up as a possibility for themselves. In optimal development the conflict is resolved as children recognize the gender-inappropriate identity to be the prerogative of the other-sex and perceive themselves unequivocally in gender-appropriate terms.

Gender-appropriate Orientations

The Oedipus complex proper is generally thought to follow this earlier period of gender-inappropriate reactions. Discussions of the Oedipus complex generally center on children's new awareness of themselves in gender-appropriate terms as masculine or feminine and the development of same-sex and cross-sex orientations in the context of their relationships to their parents.

The parents' role is anomalous in Freud's formulation of the Oedipus complex. Parents initially appear to be central but closer examination suggests a lesser role. Their particular characteristics have no part in children's subjective definitions of masculinity and femininity or in their recognition of themselves as male or female. In boys penile sensation with its active-sadistic aim is objectively male and masculine and, implicitly, is recognized as such by boys. In girls clitoral experience takes the role of penile sensation in boys. Girls' moves toward femininity by the repudiation of the mother and turn to the father are interpersonal developments, but Freud viewed them as consequent on biological factors. Girls' relationships to their parents do not determine their earlier sense of themselves as masculine nor the subsequent one of themselves as feminine. Nor do they determine girls' personal constructs of femininity. Girls' perception that they have no penis constitutes their recognition that they are female. The femininity that evolves is characterized by passivity and masochism, whatever the character of the parents. In Freud's view children's development of same-sex and cross-sex relations to their parents is the result of children's perceptions of themselves in gender terms when they become aware of sex difference, but does not involve new perceptions of their parents as masculine and feminine. It is implicit in his formulations that the parents, objectively male and female, have been so perceived by the children from the beginning. He suggests, for example, that boys' relations to their mothers, having been heterosexual since birth are not altered by oedipal phenomena. That is, recognition of sex difference does not require the boy to work our a new relation to his mother whom he now views as specifically female. Freud recognized that the form taken by the Oedipus complex was different in boys and girls but he attributed the difference to biological factors, not to the family constellation in this society with its particular roles for mothers and fathers.

The gender differentiation paradigm assigns a more substantive role to the parents in children's establishment of subjective gender definitions of same-sex and cross-sex relations. It suggests that when children become aware of sex difference they newly perceive their parents as well as themselves in gender terms. Their lifelong experience of their parents and the complex relations to them established by this time must now be integrated into perceptions of the father as specifically male, the mother as female. In children's development of subjective gender definitions the parents serve both as models of what it is to be male and female and as figures in the real world against which developing notions of masculinity and femininity can be tested. Subjective gender definitions of same-sex and cross-sex relations build on early parent-child relationships that have been objectively identificatory, same-sex and cross-sex, but have not been so defined subjectively. They occur in relationship to parents with whom children have been involved in other major developmental issues (e.g., separation-individuation) and are influenced by them. The asymmetry of these processes in girls and boys is hypothesized to be a consequence of the particular family constellations typical in this society.

The proposition that children newly perceive their parents in gender terms when they become aware of sex difference implies a significant recategorization of their notions of their parents. Now the entire array of experience with parents must be newly perceived in terms of children's developing constructs of both genital and interpersonal masculinity and femininity. When that process remains incomplete dichotomous views of parents may persist in adulthood. For instance, men may perceive women in two sharply distinct ways, as figures of ideal purity or as whores. The first appears to represent an idealized image of the pre-sex difference mother, the second the mother recognized as female.

It is in the context of their relations to their parents as representatives of the masculine and the feminine that children develop their subjective definitions of masculinity and femininity. Initially their personal gender constructs are likely to be sharply dichotomous, focusing on those characteristics that differentiate the sexes. In boys' feminine phase for example, issues of giving birth or having breasts are highlighted, not the myriad identifications with the mother that the boy does not perceive to be sex specific. Similarly, the girl in the "phallic" phase expresses precisely those characteristics she perceives to identify her father as male.

Children's notions of what it is to be masculine and feminine may be dichotomous in another respect. They may for a time identify femininity absolutely with their mothers, masculinity with their fathers. Then boys may feel that every self characteristic (self-representation, identification) derived from their mothers and in any way included in their constructs of femininity, is alien to them, girls conversely in relation to their fathers. It may be that this phenomenon of the early differentiation period is represented in notions that boys must repudiate their identifications with their mothers or disidentify with them in order to be masculine.

The differentiation paradigm suggests an alternative to repudiation of other-sex characteristics to retain one's gender identity. It suggests that tendencies toward repudiation are probably phase-appropriate during the initial differentiation period, a time when subjective gender constructs are also dichotomous. It is then or in later evocation of similar patterns that a boy might identify all procreative and nurturant activity with femininity and threatening to his sense of self as masculine. A girl, conversely, might identify professional activity or impersonality and objectivity in thought as intrinsically masculine and alien to herself as feminine. In normal development, however, these dichotomous notions are further modulated, a process that cannot occur if the repudiation of other-sex characteristics is intense. This modulation involves moves toward more realistic notions of what must be given up as the exclusive prerogative of other-sex persons. Here again the parents provide contexts for more modulated and accurate subjective gender definitions. Fathers, for example, in their nurturing and teaching roles may provide possibilities for their sons to include in their definitions of masculinity capacities first learned in identification with their mothers. Ross (1977) elaborates such processes in his discussion of the development of paternal identities in boys. Mothers, similarly, who are involved in careers, can offer girls possibilities for identifying career orientations as aspects of their feminine selves. When such integrations do not occur, men might engage in nurturant behavior and women in careers but in relatively uneasy, conflict-ridden, and defensive ways.

Differentiation theory suggests, too, that subjective definitions of same-sex and cross-sex relations build on earlier parent-child interactions in which children have not only identified with parents, or been in exclusively heterosexual (boys) or homosexual (girls) relations to their mothers. Boys have identified with their mothers but have also been treated by them in cross-sex relation to the mothers' femininity and as male to male by their fathers. Girls have been treated by mothers as same-sex persons in relation to the mothers' femaleness and femininity and by fathers in cross-sex ones as fathers ascribe femininity to them in relation to their own masculinity. With awareness of sex difference these objectively identificatory, same-sex and cross-sex relations must be subjectively defined in gender terms.

In the establishment of cross-sex relations, Freud suggested, boys have no problem. Their relations to their mothers have been heterosexual since birth and require no change in the oedipal period. Girls, once they have given up their masculine relation to their mother, their clitoral masturbation, and their wish for a penis from the father, also have no difficulty with the heterosexual relationship to the father per se. Gender differentiation theory suggests that both boys and girls have a particular set of developmental problems in the establishment of cross-sex relations to the mother and the father repectively. The optimal outcome is a relationship in which children enjoy cross-sex characteristics in relationship to the other-sex parent rather than narcissistically. For both, however, gender differentiation begins with the awareness of limit. Cross-sex parents have precisely those characteristics that children must give up as possibilities for themselves. Envy and hostility toward the parent who has what the child has not, readily occur. Moreover, as children become aware that they must cede to the other-sex parent characteristics and possibilities they have previously identified as their own, they may feel then that the parent demands from them what is rightly theirs. One outcome, if such feelings persist, is a retreat from interpersonal to narcissistic elaboration of cross-sex characteristics. Another may be represented in orientations to sexual partners in adulthood colored by feelings that the partner wishes to deprive, feelings that one must give up too much of oneself in heterosexual relationships, and by envy and vengeful wishes against the other.

In Freud's view, boys' same-sex oedipal relations are ones of rivalry with the father for the mother and subsequent identification with the father and his values. Girls' same-sex relationships to their mothers threaten them with homosexuality in which they take the male role. Normally girls repudiate their relations to their mothers because the mothers are castrated and have made the girls so. Identifications with the mother do not enter Freud's theory as contributions to girls' femininity.

The differentiation model suggests that identification and rivalry with the same-sex parent are normally involved for both boys and girls and that identification does not only occur at the close of the Oedipus complex. It suggests that before awareness of sex difference, children have established many identifications with their same-sex parents. With recognition of sex difference these must be redefined in gender terms and gradually integrated into a subjective construct of masculinity or of femininity. These form the base for the continued development of gender identification with same-sex parents. Both boys and girls may experience same-sex identifications as dangerous. To be "like" the same-sex parent may evoke fears of fusion with the other. The optimal solution, however, is not repudiation but secondary identification. The trait or capacity learned in primitive identification with the parent is integrated into one's own individual and separate self. Rivalry may be prominent at this time because it offers possibilities of both identification and separateness. Sexual rivalry between mother and daughter or father and son requires acceptance of the notion that both are of the same-sex and in the same cross-sex relation to the other parent. It encourages acute interest in the parameters of being a "female" or a "male," the better to succeed in the competition. The competition itself, however, also alleviates the danger of fusion. It is not unusual, for example, to see in a young child the sharp re-assertion of rivalry precisely at those times when tenderness with the same-sex parent or the pleasant routines of the bath or bedtime invite regression to an earlier relatively undifferentiated state.

Although differentiation theory suggests that in major ways boys and girls have similar developmental tasks in the oedipal period, in some respects their problems and the typical outcomes are not symmetrical. In Freud's view the differences are caused by the fact that the boy has a penis and the girl has none. The differentiation paradigm suggests that a major factor is the particular family constellation typical of this society, specifically the fact that the mother is the primary caregiver for both boys and girls. This family characteristic is likely to result in differing reactions in boys and girls to the initial recognition of sex difference. Girls must recognize their genital and gender differences from their fathers. The complex difficulties that may result have long been the focus of clinical investigation. Boys, however, must recognize their differences from their primary caregiver, the person who has been most central in development and most extensively represented in their self-experience. In the initial totalistic reaction boys like girls may fear that all the ways their cross-sex parent is represented in their self-experience (self representations, identifications) must be given up. Normally, this phase is transitory and children move beyond dichotomous views of masculinity and femininity. In these developments, however, boys' and girls' situations differ. Boys are likely to react intensely to their early perception that they must renounce all their self-experience derived from their mothers as alien to themselves as masculine. Moreover, during this period the mother remains the central person in their experience and a continuing reminder of what they believe they must give up as possibilities for themselves. These complexities may make it more difficult for boys than for girls to move from sharply dichotomous notions of what it is to be masculine and feminine.

Some often observed characteristics of boys and men may have their roots here. It is generally observed in both academic and clinical psychology that as early as the pre-school years boys tend to focus on masculine toys and behaviors and to avoid feminine ones and that girls are not similarly exclusive in their feminine orientations. Psychoanalytic psychologists have argued that boys must repudiate their femininity to achieve a masculine identity. In Freud's view boys, in optimum development, emerge from the Oedipus complex with a sharply delineated masculine identity and with a certain avoidance and contempt for things feminine, and no equally sharply defined feminine identity structure occurs in girls.

The prevailing interpretation of these observations is that this configuration in boys is a desirable one and that girls' failure to match it may be referred to the fact of their castration, to a developmental lag or to their reluctance to give up a wish to be a boy. The differentiation model suggests an alternative hypothesis, that a sharply delineated, narrowly masculine identity, combined with repudiation and contempt for everything feminine is not an optimal configuration in boys and men, but represents an incomplete move from the early dichotomous structure of gender definitions to a more modulated one.

The mother's centrality as caregiver for both boys and girls has differing effects on gender differentiation processes in relation to prior developmental phases as well. For both boys and girls the mother has been central in the processes of separation-individuation. For boys this may have particular effects on the establishment of cross-sex relations, for girls, on the development of same-sex ones. To boys the recognition of their gender difference from their mothers may seem another and powerful dimension of difference to be added to those required of them in separation-individuation processes. Now any regressive wishes to merge with the mother stimulate a new anxiety: to merge with the mother means the loss of masculinity. Such fears appear to be represented in perversions. Men with significant perverse development have repeatedly been observed to have major difficulties stemming from the stage of separation-individuation. In heterosexual relationships they yearn for, and fear, merging with their partners. Merging with the woman results in a desired unity and loss of painful separateness but it also means the loss of masculinity. That is, for boys separation-individuation and gender differentiation issues interpenetrate in a particular way: regressive temptations to merge with the mother threaten gender identity. To be male requires that the boy differentiate himself from her.

For girls the problem is different. Merger with the mother does not threaten their femininity. It does, however, threaten their *independent* femininity. Girls, like boys, develop their gender-defined relationships to their mothers in the context of earlier separation-individuation processes. For girls as well as boys this requires new dimensions of separation, though of a less visible sort. In the separation-individuation processes girls have normally made major progress in establishing themselves as individuals distinct from their mothers. Now they must perceive themselves as both like their mothers in gender and distinct from them as individuals. They must establish secondary identifications with their mothers as feminine in which attributes previously shared with their mothers in a two-person unity now become depersonified aspects of their individual feminine selves distinct from but related to the mother whose way of being feminine is her own. Each of the secondary identifications represents a separation. The developmental danger is of a regressive return to the more primitive identification and relationship of a two-person feminine unity with the mother.

One reaction, to avoid the dangers of both fusion with the mother and separation from her, is the repudiation of the mother and turn to the father. Freud viewed this as necessary for the development of an appropriate femininity. Differentiation theory suggests that it makes such development impossible. Its apparent function is to avoid the threat of fusion with the mother. Its less overt one is to avoid the separation that occurs when secondary identifications replace more primitive ones. Repudiation leaves the primitive identifications and the fusion with the mother intact. The femininity in relation to the father is likely to be narrowly female, focused on ways in which the female is in cross-sex relation to the male, but not enriched by the integration of identifications with the mother.

An alternative and perhaps more common reaction may be an incomplete replacement of primitive identifications with the mother by secondary ones. Then the development of an appropriate gender identity in identification with the mother may appear to occur, but in fact be dominated by primitive identifications in which the shared attribute represents the girl's participation in a two-person unity with the mother. In such cases the integration and modulation of self-representations as feminine into a coherent gender identity cannot occur. The girl's sense of her genitals as the bodily center of her independent femininity is likely to be incomplete. Her same-sex relations to her mother are not those of two individuals with distinct organizations of their femininity. Her cross-sex relations to her father are not her own and independent of those the mother has with him.

SUMMARY

Gender differentiation theory suggests that the observations Freud subsumed under his concept of the Oedipus complex can be understood as products of gender differentiation processes, specifically the establishment of subjective definitions of bodily and social masculinity and femininity, self-definition in gender terms, and the elaboration of same-sex and cross-sex relations newly defined in gender terms.

It suggests that the processes of this period are initiated by children's interest in sex difference, not by biological changes in penile or clitoral sensation. The observed intensification of interest in the genitals is not due to physical changes but to children's involvement in categorizing their genitals in gender terms. The restructuring of children's relations to their parents is not the product of a biologically patterned Oedipus complex. It is the result of children's new perceptions of both themselves and their parents in gender terms, and the consequent elaboration of same-sex and cross-sex relations to them as specifically masculine and feminine in relation to the children's own masculinity or femininity.

REFERENCES

Abraham, K. (1920). Manifestations of the female castration complex. In K. Abraham, *Selected Papers on Psychoanalysis.* New York: Basic Books, 1927.

Block, J. H. (1973). Conceptions of sex role. *American Psychological.* 28: 512–526.

Boehm, E. (1930). The femininity-complex in men. *Int. J. Psychoanal.* 11: 444–469.

Galenson, E. & Roiphe, H. (1977). Some suggested revisions concerning early female development. In H. P. Blum, ed. *Female Psychology,* New York: Int. Univ. Press.

Greenacre, P. (1953). Certain relationships between fetishism and faculty development in the body image. *Psychoanal. Study Child,* 8: 79–98.

Greenacre, P. (1968). Perversions: general considerations regarding their genetic and dynamic background. *Psychoanal. Study Child,* 23: 47–62.

Greenson, R. R. (1968). Dis-identifying with the mother, its special importance for the boy. *Int. J. Psychoanal.* 49: 370–373.

Jacobson, E. (1976). Ways of female superego formation and the female castration conflict. *Psycho-Anal. Quart.* 45: 525. [Translated from Int. Z Psycho-Anal. 1937, 23, 402.]

Kestenberg, J. S. (1968). Outside and inside, male and female. *J. Amer. Psychoanal. Assoc.* 16: 457–520.

Kleeman, J. A. (1966). Genital self-discovery during a boy's second year. *Psychoanal. Study Child,* 21: 358–392.

Maccoby, E. E. & Jacklin, C. U. (1974), *The psychology of sex differences.* Stanford University Press.

Mead, M (1967). *Male and female.* New York: Wm. Morrow and Co.

Parens, H., Pollock, L., Stern, J., & Kramer, S. (1977). On the girl's entry into the oedipus complex. In H. P. Blum, ed. *Female Psychology,* New York: International Universities Press.

Rado, W. (1933). Fear of castration in women. *Psychoanal. Quart.* 2: 425–475.

Ross, J. M. (1977). Towards fatherhood: the epigenesis of paternal identity during a boy's first decade. *Int. Rev. Psychoanal.*, 4: 327–347.

Socarides, C. W. (1960). The development of a fetishistic perversion. *J. Amer. Psychoanal. Assoc.*, 8: 281–311.

Stoller, R. J. (1968), *Sex and gender.* Jason Aronson.

5 A Differentiation Model of Identity Development

INTRODUCTION

This chapter proposes a model for the development of identity generally, into which gender identity fits as a special case. The term identity has a general use but it has not yet found a place in which its relationships to other concepts in psychological theory are clear. As Schafer (1968) points out, identity has not been adequately defined in relation to other terms like self, ego, social role, personality, or character. Discussions of identity are in general agreement that notions of identity and its development should be explored from all possible vantage points (e. g., development through psychosexual and psychosocial stages, relations to such notions as id, ego, and superego, development and patterning of identifications and object relations, the influence of social forces) and that such explorations are only in their beginning stages.

Here, aspects of identity development are traced from hypothesized roots in primary narcissism. Objectively, it is proposed, infants' experience (e.g., grasping, nursing) can be observed to occur in interaction with the environment. Subjectively, however, infants themselves have not differentiated between their experiencing (thought, perception, need) and that which is being experienced (thought about, perceived, etc.). They equate their experience with reality. It follows that they are subject to two illusions, that of omnipotence (the notion that one's own experiencing (cognition) carries with it the relevant reality) and that of primary creativity (the notion that events exist only as they are being experienced). Narcissistic experience is hypothesized to occur in relatively discrete units (events) composed of an aspect of self in interaction with aspects of the environment (as when the child's grasp of the father's finger constitutes the event). The self is central (though without a *sense* of self) in bringing events into subjective existence and, within events, in determining which aspects of the environment are called into reality. Borderline identity structure is hypothesized to manifest residues of narcissistic experiencing conceptualized in this way, in tendencies toward illusions of omnipotence and primary creativity, the organization of experience into relatively discrete units and a concomitant use of splitting for defensive purposes, the part-object character of relationships with others and their embeddedness in these experience units, and the sense of personal centrality both in bringing events into existence and, within events, in determining which aspects of the environment are to have reality.

The transition out of narcissism is hypothesized to be made possible by a gradual differentiation of self and non-self out of undifferentiated experience. That differentiation culminates at about age two in the capacity for symbolic thought (thought independent of its referents), and a corresponding recognition of a universe independent of self. The sense of omnipotence is differentiated into intention (self) and causality (non-self), and primary creativity into thought (self) and that which is thought about (non-self). Other differentiations follow the same pattern, among them self-other unity into self and other, and the gender-undifferentiated sense of self into a recognition of self as sex-specific in relation to other-sex persons. In the course of these developments event-centered identity experience becomes increasingly sophisticated. Self, increasingly experienced in delimited terms as a center of thought and intention, as individual and sex-specific, now interacts with a world recognized as independent of self and governed by impersonal causality, and other persons recognized as distinct from self and as sex-specific.

These developments also make possible a second mode of identity experience. The capacity for symbolic thought and the concurrent recognition of a world independent of self make possible intrapsychic conflict and reality testing. The categories of reality external to the self become the standard against which self aspects (as also other aspects of experience) are tested. In the resulting identity mode it is not self that is central in relation to an external world. In this mode the categories of external reality (physical ones such as height, social ones such as daughter or brother, etc.) are the standards to which even the self is subject. It is an allocentric mode of identity experience, here called category-centered, in contrast to the autocentric, event-centered one.

It is *not* hypothesized, however, that this new mode of identity experience *replaces* the event-centered one. Rather than a linear development from narcissistic (event-centered) to postnarcissistic (category-centered) modes of identity experience, it is proposed that a bimodal identity organization develops in which event-centered and category-centered identity modes may occur at equally high levels of sophistication. The two modes provide an autocentric and an allocentric aspect to identity experience. One is experience in the particular, the other experience of self in the context of the general. One is a sense of self as center of thought and will, the other of self subordinated to an objective system of categories. One is self as center of experience, the other is self as one among many. One is likely to have ready access to emotion, intuition, and the evocation of particular events, the other to rational analysis. In one context, an experience may more readily be expressed by metaphor, poetry, or drama, in the other, by prose and the orderly presentation of argument.

IDENTITY STRUCTURE IN THE NARCISSISTIC PERIOD

It is generally accepted within psychoanalytic psychology that the earliest sense of identity is rooted in the period of infantile narcissism. In Freud's terms (Freud, 1914) it is a sense of being "the center and core of creation." Freud conceptualized this centrality of self in a particular way. Children's experience, he suggested, is directed to the interior of the body and is characterized by illusions of omnipotence. The sense organs are not cathected and consciousness is not attached to them. Motor activity consists of affective discharge. It is not action directed toward the alteration of reality. The transition out of narcissism begins at about two years of age. It involves a shift in the focus of interest from the body interior to the external world, a cathexis of the sense organs and the beginning of purposive action directed toward the alteration of reality. This shift in orientation (toward the external world) and in the functions of motor activity (toward instrumental action) results in a comprehensive new organization of thought and experience whose parameters are reflected in notions of the transition from pleasure to reality ego, primary to secondary process thought, and narcissism to object-relatedness.

Elsewhere, in a footnote (Freud, 1911), Freud suggests that this formulation of infantile narcissism is schematic and must not be taken altogether literally because an organism that totally neglected the outside world could not function for even the briefest time. Nevertheless, he believed "this fiction" to reflect the child's actual situation if one took the mother-child pair as the narcissistic unit.

Subsequent theoretical formulations based on both clinical investigation and direct observation have viewed the child's relation to the mother as a major aspect of its interaction with the environment rather than as part of a narcissistic unit. In these perspectives the infant's experience is conceptualized as occurring in interaction with the environment from the time of birth, and as involved from the beginning in mutual adjustments with others (e.g., in nursing), and accomodations to the nonhuman environment (e.g., in grasping or visual tracking) that are "actions directed toward the alteration of reality."

From such modified perspectives the conception of narcissistic experience and of the transition out of narcissism must be seen in a new light. If the infant is actively engaged with the environment, how can its experience properly be called narcissistic? If the self is not central in the sense that experience is directed toward the interior of the body (or the mother-child unit), in what sense can it be seen as central? If illusions of omnipotence and primary creativity are a part of narcissism, how can they be viewed as occurring in the context of adaptive behavior? If the change in identity organization at about age two can no longer be conceptualized as a shift in the focus of experience from the body interior to the external world and in the function of activity from affect discharge to purposive action, how can it usefully be viewed?

An Alternative Paradigm for Narcissistic Identity Organization

Hypotheses derived from psychoanalytic investigation and Piaget's theory set the stage for a revised formulation of narcissistic identity organization that promises to be responsive to these problems. It is proposed here that from the beginning, the infant's experiences (e.g., nursing, grasping, visual focusing) objectively occur in active and adaptive interaction with its environment. Subjectively, however, the infant is not aware of interacting with a stable world independent of itself. In its own experience, only that *is* which is within immediate experience (an incident of grasping, of nursing). In Freud's terms (1925), the experience itself is the guarantor of reality. In Piaget's (1951), the world of the infant is one in which objects continually come into being as a result of the infant's actions (grasping, seeing) and subside into non-existence with the termination of the experience.

This form of experience can be seen to have particular characteristics. Individual experiences are relatively discrete from one another. The unit of experience is the-infant-in-interaction-with-the-environment. For convenience sake these units will be called *events*. Within each unit or event the infant is actively engaged in mutual adjustment with others or accommodation to non-human actualities. In terms of identity organization these notions imply that the narcissistic identity is composed of identity units relatively unintegrated with one another. The unit of identity experience is not a self representation or an identification but is, objectively, an object relation: an experience of self in interaction with the environment. In each event (e.g., the infant grasping the parent's finger) an aspect of self is involved with an aspect of the environment: it is a relation of part objects.

In such experience the self is central in two ways. In the earliest period of life only "experiencing" is known to the infant. All existence, therefore, is perceived as a function of this "experiencing." The infant is in this way absolutely central, though without a *sense* of its centrality. Within events the infant is central as well. It is its own experience (grasping, etc.) that determines which aspects of the human or nonhuman environment are included in a given event. In identity terms this implies that a narcissistic identity experience is one in which the infant has no sense that anything can occur independent of his own experiencing and in which only those aspects of the environment relevant to his actualization of an event will have reality for him.

This "experiencing," moreover, provides the foundation for the illusions of omnipotence and primary creativity. (The term primary creativity seems to better reflect the situation in which events are sensed to exist only when they are being experienced than does the more commonly used term omniscience.) In narcissistic "experiencing" infants cannot think beyond the present event: cognition is limited to the current actuality. Therefore, on the one hand, whatever is thought is accompanied by the relevant reality, and on the other, objects cannot be known to continue in existence when they are not being perceived. The illusion of the omnipotence of thought has its roots in the first of these, the illusion of primary creativity in the second. Before thought can occur independently of its referents (that which is thought about) the awareness that thought does not carry with it the relevant actuality is not possible. Before objects can be perceived to be permanently in existence independent of one's involvement with them, no notion that they are not dependent on one's experiencing for their existence can occur. In other words, notions of omnipotence and primary creativity can, at this point in development, be equated with narcissistic experiencing; the first focusing on cognition (its capacity to carry actuality with it), the second on objective reality (its existence as dependent on the infant's experiencing). In this formulation illusions of omnipotence and primary creativity do not accompany narcissism. They are its components: the infant's narcissistic experience is experience in which cognition is accompanied by the actuality to which it refers and actualities are perceived to exist only when they are being experienced.

In summary, the hypothesis that infants initially live within their immediate experience, and the corollary, that the infant perceives all existence to be a function of its experiencing, yields a conception of infantile narcissism consistent with current notions of infant development. The infant is viewed as actively engaged in mutual adjustments with or accommodations to its human and non-human environment. Its experience occurs in relatively discrete units (events) composed of a self aspect interacting with environmental part objects. Self is central (though without a *sense* of self). "Experiencing" brings events into being, and within events it is the activity of the self (grasping, sucking) that determines which aspects of the environment are called into existence. Moreover, because the infant's experiencing does not initially differentiate cognition and actuality (thought and the referents of thought) the illusion of omnipotence (the notion that any cognition is accompanied by the relevant actuality) and primary creativity (the notion that an object's existence depends on one's experiencing it) are integral to narcissistic experiencing.

From the first days of life, modifications occur in this absolute narcissism that increase the complexity and integration of narcissistic experience and also set the stage for the identity re-organization that begins at about age two. Two directions of development can be distinguished for purposes of analysis.

The first concerns the integration of self aspects and aspects of objects (part-selves and part-objects) and their differentiation out of the undifferentiated experience of events. The earliest form of organization occurs as similar events (e.g., of grasping) are repeated over and over again; that is, by the assimilation of successive infant-in-interaction-with-the-environment units into increasingly complex constellations (schemes) that are themselves relatively unintegrated with one another. Gradually integrations of self (as of objects) occur across event constellations as well. As self aspects embedded in discrete event constellations occur together, they are integrated with one another. For example, when the infant has established event constellations of visual tracking and of grasping, it begins to be able to grasp the object it sees (e.g., a plastic ring). In this process, self aspects (oneself as see-er and as grasp-er) achieve a beginning integration. Such integration also begins to decrease the embeddedness of self (and similarly of objects) in specific events. When, for example, the infant self as "seer–grasper" is involved in a grasp event, the self is not now a totally undifferentiated aspect of that event: self-as-seer, now an integral self aspect, provides the self with a measure of independence. In Piaget's terms "objectification" is beginning. Gradually, as these integrations and differentiations continue, the part-selves and part-objects of primitive narcissistic experience become increasingly complex organizations, although before the transition out of narcissism becomes focal there is little possibility for integrating discrepant or incompatible self (or object) constellations with one another and the definitive establishment of a whole self and whole objects.

   The second direction of development concerns differentiation of primary creativity into thought and the objects of thought, and of omnipotence into intention and causality. Piaget traces relevant infantile developments. He observes that at six months of age an infant's excited interest in an object (e.g., a toy duck) instantly vanishes when the object is no longer within experience (is lost from view). However, at nine months, the infant hunts for the duck when it is removed from sight. This behavior signals the beginning of differentiation out of primary creativity. To hunt for a hidden duck requires that the duck have existence for the infant even when it is not within direct experience (is lost from view). One product of this differentiation, therefore, is a gradual development of a world of objects independent of one's experience of them (in thought, perception, wish, etc.). The other differentiation product is thought which is no longer tied to the immediate present reality. To hunt for a non-visible duck requires that cognition be able to deal with an object in its (at first momentary) absence. Thought in the absence of its referents (symbolic thought) is beginning to be established. To be able to cognize phenomena without their presence in reality and to know that objects continue to exist when they are outside one's experience of them undermines the illusion that all existence is a function of one's experience (the illusion of primary creativity).

Concurrently, foundations are being laid for the differentiation of the illusion of omnipotence into intention and events governed by impersonal causality. Piaget observes distinct signs of intention at about six months. Rather than self as an undifferentiated part of an event. (e.g., watching a mobile suspended from the carriage top), the infant may now make a particular body movement or gesture (e.g., a wriggle of the torso) and look attentively for results (the dancing of the mobile). Intention is being differentiated out of undifferentiated experiencing and to some extent being distinguished from the object of intention. At this time objects are still "action objects," subjectively functions of the infant's own experiencing and without their own intrinsic modes of action. However, in subsequent months infants show increasing interest in objects as having their own actions (swinging, moving on an inclined plane, rolling). As the infant increasingly distinguishes phenomena that are governed by impersonal rules from those responsive to his intention or will, the illusion of omnipotence, that all phenomena are governed by his active experiencing (later, his intentions), is called into question.

These developments spell the eventual end of narcissistic experiencing. The processes of objectification gradually terminate primitive narcissistic experience embedded in discrete events in which self and other are undifferentiated part objects. Illusions of primary creativity and omnipotence, here considered the hallmarks of narcissism, are undermined. These same developments also lay the foundation for a transition to a post-narcissistic identity organization. Thought, increasingly independent of its referents (symbolic thought), will provide a necessary tool for the recognition and resolution of conflict. The increasing integration of self and objects will bring inconsistencies to light that require resolution. And the subjective establishment of a stable world of realities independent of oneself will provide the standard against which conflicts can be tested.

Some Residues of the Narcissistic Identity Organization in Borderline Disorders

This formulation of narcissistic identity organization shows promise of contributing to the clarification of some repeatedly observed (but not fully understood) characteristics of varied groups of individuals clinically observed to show similar organizations of self structure and object relations. They include as-if personalities (Deutsch, 1942), persons with "screen identities" (Greenacre, 1958), imposters (Deutsch, 1955; Greenacre, 1958), schizoid personalities Khan, 1960), and borderline adults (Kernberg, 1966) and children (Fast & Chethik, 1976). Individuals in these groups have been seen to have particular difficulties in self structure and object relations. Narcissistic characteristics are prominent (e.g., illusions of omnipotence and primary creativity, disturbances in the sense of reality). There are indications that their character organizations reflect the dominance of a period prior to children's entry into the oedipal period, and that splitting rather than repression is their predominant defensive mode. A degree of similarity among the groups is suggested by their all having been referred to as borderline or schizoid, or to have personality organizations akin to those, though the continuing imprecision of those terms warns against too great an assumption of common structure on that basis.

The identity experience of individuals in these groups seems to be more readily comprehended in terms of the formulations proposed here than in terms of Freud's formulation that narcissistic experience is directed toward the interior of the body (or mother-child unit), without cathexis of the outside world.

A major clinical observation, variously expressed, is that the identity experience of individuals in these groups is unintegrated. The character of this lack of integration seems to be congruent with the notion of discrete identity constellations proposed here. Kernberg (1966), for example, notes that the object relations of individuals with borderline disorders are composed of fragmented self-other bonds, each of which is an entire transference paradigm. Khan (1960) describes schizoid persons as projecting "pieces of incomplete experiences" which are "congealed into operational unities." In clinical work, he warns, the therapist may be gratified at the rapidity and completeness with which such a patient accepts an interpretation, perceives its implications, and expresses them in his behavior, attitudes, and affective orientation, only to find that this whole organization is a discrete identity constellation existing side by side with the previous neurotic one and in no way modifying it. Deutsch (1942), discussing as-if personalities, appears to be observing a similar phenomenon. One of her patients, an artist, adopted very quickly and totally, the style and mode of perception of her teacher, but when she became the student of another teacher her adoption of his very different approach was equally total and rapid. No trace of the previous orientation remained: the two identities remained discrete.

This form of identity experience does not appear to reflect a self absorbtion derived from experience directed to the interior of the body or the self without interest in the environment. It appears to be more usefully conceptualized as being built on a foundation of discrete self-in-interaction-with-the-environment units. Kernberg has been most explicit in emphasizing that in borderline patients the unit of experience is a dyad, composed of self and other joined by a motive or an affect, and that such units may be elaborated into larger organizations, each of which, in therapy, is "a complete transference paradigm." Khan and Deutsch do not describe the discrete identity constellations to which they refer as being composed of self-other units, but Khan's description appears to be consonant with Kernberg's of discrete transference paradigms, and Deutsch's seems to imply or at least be congruent with the notion of specific environmental contexts within which discrete identity organizations are elaborated.

The proposed formulation suggests an aspect of this organization of experience beyond that proposed by Kernberg. Based on the hypothesis that in infantile "experiencing," self and that which is independent of self (other persons and the non-human environment) are initially undifferentiated parts of the event, it would suggest that not only self and other, but the non-human environment as well, are included in the experience units of the later narcissistic identity structure. Among adults seen therapeutically, the dyadic experience unit is likely to be most evident though even in such cases the non-human environment may "set the stage" for expression of a particular identity constellation. It is common to find, for example, that a particular piece of clothing—a flashy scarf, a hat worn at a rakish angle, a large ring—may serve to evoke a particular identity; or that a particular locale—the office, home—may do so. In Deutsch's (1955) imposter patient, non-human aspects of the environment played a pronounced part in his elaboration of his sense of identity.

In more seriously disturbed individuals, experience may more closely approach primitive "experiencing" in which self and other are not objectified but are relatively undifferentiated aspects of the event as a whole. In a young boy, Gary, so severely disturbed (diagnosis: borderline) as to require in-patient treatment in mid-childhood, such an experience structure could be observed at times with particular clarity. A highlight of Gary's week was his parents' visit that took place in the dayroom of his living unit at a particular day and time each week. On one occasion, when his parents were unable to come for the scheduled visit, Gary became increasingly frantic as the time for the visit-to-be-missed approached. Suddenly he had a "terrific idea." The Emersons, who lived on his street in his home town, could come. Then he could have his parents' visit. It became clear that he had no particular attachment to the Emersons. However, if these stand-ins came from his street, in his home town, and were there at the regular hour, for the allotted period of time, in the dayroom, his parents' visit could happen in its appointed way and his sense of being utterly lost would be gone, though in fact he would not have seen his parents. The parents' visit, it became clear, was an experience unit in which he, his parents and the non-human environment were all aspects, but neither his own individuality (as son in relation to his actual parents) or that of his parents (for whom the Emersons might substitute) was of central importance to the event as a whole.

The narcissistic illusion of omnipotence in such persons is not readily understood in terms of a sense of one's (internal) wish having effects on (external) reality. It appears to be more usefully conceptualized as a requirement that one's "experiencing" determine the reality, rather than the post-narcissistic converse, that one adjusts one's ideas and plans to realities independent of oneself.

In Gary's projected parents' visit, for example, it was imperative that it be his experience that determined the actuality. He was not able to adapt himself to the reality of a potential visit with the Emersons as friends of the family, acceptable as visitors but quite other than his parents. The actuality was required to match his "experiencing:" The Emerson's role was limited to that of stand-ins for his parents. The observation that persons with borderline disorders do not act toward others in terms of the other person's particular character, but as a prop for projection seems to refer to the same phenomenon. However, the proposed paradigm would suggest that the use of the object as a prop for projection is part of a larger phenomenon. It would suggest that an internally created self-in-interaction-with-other is being played out, with a particular self-aspect in relation to an aspect of the other whose participation is limited to the function imagined by the self (as the Emerson's role would have been Gary's parents' visit).

The proposed paradigm suggests, further, that in narcissistic experience the sense of identity resides in the event as a whole, rather than in a stable self structure independent of the particular event in which the individual is engaged. Some support of this notion as it applies clinically is offered by experiences of identity loss in borderline disorders. Greenacre (1958), in her study of imposters, emphasizes that the enactment of an imposturous identity requires the participation of relevant others, and that if the enactment is disrupted by their non-acceptance, the result is a loss of the sense of reality and identity. It seems likely that one of Deutsch's "as-if" patients was expressing a similar sense of identity loss when, after her imposturous identity as psychoanalyst was shattered by Deutsch's refusal to accept it, she is quoted as saying "I am so empty! My God, I am so empty! I have no feelings!" Less vivid reactions can often be observed clinically. When the therapist interrupts the actualization of an identity constellation (e.g., one enacted with the therapist) the patient may feel "detached," "distant," or "unrelated," an experience which, on investigation, can often be seen to be an experience of threat to the sense of identity.

The part-object nature of self, other, and aspects of the non-human environment in these experience units is readily observed clinically. Deutsch's painter patient shows two part-selves discrete from one another. The self-aspects in the relatively unintegrated dyads Kernberg describes are not integrated into a whole self. Correspondingly, the other person in the experience unit is a part object. Only those aspects of the other (the painting teacher, the "other" of Kernberg's dyad, the Emersons) relevant to the event are experienced as existing while the experience lasts.

Finally, integration *across* event-based constellations is missing or disturbed. The part-object nature of self, others, and the non-human environment implies such lack of integration. Gary, again, provides a particularly vivid example. On one occasion, due to special family plans, Gary was to go home with his parents at the time of his regular parents' visit. Gary's delight at the trip home was great. However, in his therapy, pleasure alternated in his play with images of self as abandoned boy, or a lost and hungry dog with no parents. It became clear that these fantasies reflected his sense of abandonment due to the missed parents' visit. The fact that at the very time of his regular visit with his parents he would instead be snugly in the car with them and going home, could not allay his increasingly frantic sense of being abandoned. The happy-boy-in-car-with-parents event could not be integrated with the boy-without-a-parents'-visit event. In response to his therapist's efforts to help him in the integration process he could offer only the desperate suggestion that when his parents came to pick him up they first spend the allotted time in the dayroom having a parents' visit, *then* go home in the car. He could not sustain more than momentarily the idea of a unitary self, himself as being with his parents in one of two ways, either in the dayroom or in the car, but in neither case abandoned.

THE TRANSITION OUT OF NARCISSISTIC IDENTITY EXPERIENCE

In Freud's view (and that generally accepted in psychoanalytic psychology) the transition out of narcissism represents a change from the infant's experiential focus on inner body processes to a focus on an environment external to itself. It is associated with a transition from primary to secondary process thought (eventually to the capacity for thought independent of its referents and categorical thought), and results in reality testing whose consequences may be experienced as narcissistic losses.

The formulation being developed here has implications for each of these phenomena but organizes them differently. It proposes that the infant interacts actively and adaptively with its environment from birth. Narcissism is seen to be a mode of understanding one's experience rather than a particular focus of experience (the interior of the body). The transition out of narcissism, correspondingly, is not seen to be a change in the focus of experience (a newly discovered external world) but a cognitive re-organization. It represents the culmination of processes beginning at birth, particularly the subjective establishment of a stable external world, the growing capacity for symbolic thought, and the integration of part-selves and part-objects into increasingly complex wholes.

These developments make intrapsychic conflict and reality testing both necessary and possible. In narcissistic experience whatever is experienced *is*. The question of reality testing does not arise. In Freud's terms (1925) the experience itself is the guarantor of reality. Intrapsychic conflict does not occur. An experience that is discrepant from others is not adduced to the established constellation (scheme) of events but begins the formation of a new and discrete one. That is, in narcissistic experiencing the predominant mode of dealing with discrepancy is the formation of discrete event constellations. Splitting, the defensive mode commonly found in borderline and allied disorders, appears to have its developmental origins here. Khan's description of the patient's formation of an entire constellation of feelings, attitudes, and relations to others on the basis of an interpretation is illustrative. The therapist's pointing out of discrepancies did not result in conflict and possible change. It resulted in the elaboration of a new constellation without effect on the old one.

The integration of self aspects (and other event components) across incompatible events and constellations requires a mode of resolving discrepancies. Symbolic thought, which makes it possible to bring to mind more than one notion at a time, makes intrapsychic comparisons and conflict possible. When two or more contrary notions can be experienced (thought) simultaneously, "experiencing" can no longer be the "guarantor of reality." A new standard is found in the established sense of mental reality independent of one's experience. Now, aspects of the environment can no longer be brought into existence as they are required for the actualization of an event and dropped from existence when the event is over. Instead, the environment itself (consensually validated reality) becomes the standard against which an idea is tested. In other words, a shift gradually takes place from self as central and its "experiencing" as the arbiter of reality, to the dimensions of consensually validated reality as the standard and even self as subject to its dictates.

It is against these standards that conflicts among part-selves and part-objectives are resolved. When the discrepancies or contradictions among aspects of others or of the non-human environment (e.g., visual paradoxes, discrepancies of size or weight) they present puzzles for resolution. When they involve the self they may involve intrapsychic conflict as well, that is, an unwillingness to accept the dictates of reality. Then the outcome may be a partial giving up of the integration process (a regression to splitting), resolution of the conflict in favor of consensually validated reality, or repression which implies a break in an otherwise synthesized organization.

Narcissistic loss reactions appear to be typical early accompaniments of the identity re-organization processes. The proposed paradigm suggests that they result from the reality testing of the discrepant notions that all existence is a function of one's own experience and those representing the recognition that valued aspects of reality are independent of oneself. Before the integrative processes now beginning, these incompatible notions can co-exist without mutual interference. It is the integrative processes that result in the recognition that discrepancy exists, and that the notion of self as arbiter of all existence is untenable. The initial reaction to the recognition that valued aspects of existence are independent of self is a sense of loss. To the extent that experience still occurs as discrete events, any loss is necessarily experienced as total, and to the extent that identity still resides in the event as a whole the loss is experienced as a loss of identity.

The integrative processes also provide the means for resolving these loss reactions. The earlier establishment of experience that objectively takes self and what is independent of self into account provides the base for the new subjective organization of experience. As self representations become integrated with one another, a loss experience in the context of one event is no longer experienced as total loss. And as the sense of identity increasingly resides in the self as a whole rather than in the event, single events become less able to result in feelings of identity loss.

When development does not occur optimally, however, narcissistic loss reactions may persist into later life. They occur as feelings of loss in relation to the sense of self as arbiter of all existence. They are precipitated by a recognition that some valued aspect of reality is independent of oneself. They are expressed in a sense of utter loss, basically a loss of self or identity. They may occur in any identity-relevant area of experience in which recognition is required that an aspect of reality is independent of self. Significant among these are the loss of the illusions of omnipotence and primary creativity, the sense of other persons as distinct from oneself, and the recognition of sex difference. Denial of the relevant limit of the self occurs in the re-assertion of the self as arbiter of all existence.

Castration Anxiety as a Narcissistic Loss Reaction

This formulation provides a new context within which to understand the phenomena of castration anxiety. Generally the castration anxiety attendant on recognition of sex difference has been explored in the context of the theory of psychosexual development. Focus has been on its relation to prior oral and anal stages and subsequent oedipal ones. The present context, that of the transition out of narcissism, provides an additional perspective (though not a substitutive one).

Issues of narcissism have not been altogether absent from discussions of castration anxiety. The point in development (about age two) at which recognition of sex difference and castration anxiety occur is the same as that postulated for major transitions out of narcissism. In Freud's thinking about narcissism the transition from it to object relatedness marks the entry into the oedipal period, and in his formulation of psychosexual development the oedipal period begins with the recognition of sex difference. Castration anxiety in men is generally recognized to represent a narcissistic loss reaction though it is not always clear whether the term as used in a particular context refers simply to a bodily loss or also includes reactions concerned with the centrality of self, omnipotence, and so forth. In women, it has been hypothesized (e.g., by Torok, 1970), that the loss reaction focuses on the penis but has meanings that represent the loss of such illusory narcissistic characteristics as never being disappointed, having no obstacles to success, not being subject to natural or social law, and so on. Alternatively, fears related to loss of omnipotence and primary creativity are observed to accompany castration anxiety and are hypothesized to be displacements of it. Despite this generally recognized association of narcissism and castration anxiety their relation has not been the focus of systematic examination in terms of the move from self-involvement to object-relatedness, primary to secondary process thought, and pleasure to reality ego.

To do so in the context of the proposed paradigm puts some clinical observations in a new context and suggests some new directions for exploration. These cannot be examined here in detail but some of their dimensions can be indicated.

The recognition of sex difference and castration anxiety are not viewed here as consequent on a biologically based increase in awareness of the genitals but on a cognitive reorganization. During the narcissistic period children learn about many characteristics of males and females. They do not yet exclude any of these as possibilities for themselves. Their notions of themselves as "boy" or "girl" are not yet delimited. The *recognition* of sex difference, made possible by their new cognitive abilities, signals the transition out of narcissism in the area of sex and gender. Children become aware that the notion that all sex and gender possibilities are open to them is incompatible with the notion of self as girl or boy and that it must be given up.

This recognition is the product of significant developmental accomplishment. It implies that the organization of self aspects into a whole self has proceeded far enough that notions of self having unlimited sex and gender potential can no longer co-exist with the notion of self as girl or boy. Sufficient development must have occurred of a sense of an environment independent of one's own experiencing to permit reality testing. Enough capacity for symbolic thought must have been established to make possible the recognition of a discrepancy between narcissistic notions of unlimited possibility and notions that recognize the impossibility of having other-sex attributes, to require a resolution of that discrepancy, to make the judgment that the narcissistic notion must be given up, and to suffer (and in some way resolve) whatever conflict ensues.

The loss reaction itself is hypothesized to be a narcissistic loss of a kind that occurs in all areas in which children must recognize valued aspects of existence to be independent of themselves. Among these the area of sex and gender is a major one. Other persons (e.g., the mother) as independent of self is another. Self as center of intention in relation to impersonal causality, and as thinker in relation to an independent reality are others. In this view, therefore, narcissistic losses may or may not be bodily losses though they are in every case losses to the self.

This formulation also suggests an altered context for the observation that notions of loss of omnipotence and primary creativity tend to accompany castration anxiety. They are seen neither as displacements of castration anxiety nor as the more basic anxiety that underlies a relatively epiphenomenal castration anxiety. They are instead seen to be narcissistic loss reactions in their own right.

In any of the narcissistic loss reactions observed clinically several foci of loss may be represented and any one may substitute defensively for another. For example, in the severely disturbed Gary, sharp reactions to lost omnipotence had little to do with castration anxiety but often involved intense narcissistically experienced separation anxiety triggered by evidence that the other (e.g., the therapist) was independent of himself. In one adult patient explicitly narcissistic reactions to object loss (e.g., the therapist's absence) tended to have large admixtures of "castration" anxiety and felt loss of primary creativity. In another, actual body damage (minor surgery) evoked a whole array of narcissistic loss reactions including castration anxiety, fury at others for being independent of self, fears of utter incapacity for creative thought, and angry assertions of omnipotence.

The narcissistic loss reaction in relation to recognition of sex difference (castration anxiety) is hypothesized to have a structure also shared by other narcissistic losses. It occurs as a recognition that self is not the arbiter of all reality; it is felt as a total loss, centrally a loss of identity; and denial of the loss occurs in the re-assertion that all existence is a function of one's own experiencing. The sense of total loss in castration anxiety, in narcissistic reaction to object loss, and in feelings of lost omnipotence or primary creativity has been widely observed. Its character as an identity loss has been less widely recognized though some relevant observations are available. In the area of primary creativity and omnipotence the sense of lost identity when a narcissistic creation fails is very evident. Greenacre (1958) and Deutsch (1955) speak of it as occurring when an imposture fails; there are indications of it in as-if personalities; and in Gary it was readily observed when a narcissistically created event failed to materialize (Fast, 1974). Narcissistic reactions to object loss triggered by separation from or loss of another person may be expressed in feelings of depersonalization in which the sense of threat to identity may also be revived (Fast & Chethik, 1976). In the area of sex- and gender-related narcissistic loss (castration anxiety) the sense of lost identity has less often been noted. However, in some cases, when the focus is castration anxiety the sense of threat to identity becomes clear. At times it lies behind statements of "utter loss" or that the loss is "total." At other times patients may speak more clearly of feelings of deadness, of being or having nothing worthwhile, of being "wiped out" or "swallowed by a hole in space," which on exploration can be seen to be experiences of threat to identity. Whether loss of identity (or threat of it) underlies castration anxiety in all cases of sex difference, related castration anxiety must await further evidence.

Finally, denials of loss occur in a re-assertion of the self as arbiter of all reality. In the areas of omnipotence and primary creativity the strenuous assertion of self as central to reality can be observed in imposters' increasingly frantic demands that the reality conform to the image they have created and in other disorders generally referred to as borderline as well. In denial of narcissistic object loss the attempts to coerce the other, to see the other as acting, or having acted exactly as one had predicted, and so forth have been extensively explored. The re-assertion of unlimited sex and gender potential in denial of "castration" is implied in the proposed paradigm. It seems also to be the case that when denial occurs in one content area regression occurs in the others as well. Experiences of the others as no more than a conduit for the expression of one's own will tend to be accompanied by notions of omnipotence; denials of sex difference tend to be accompanied by illusions of omnipotence and denials that others are separate from self, and so forth.

DIFFERENTIATION PROPER

In the subsequent identity-relevant developments implied by this model a bimodal organization of identity is established. The first aspect retains the event-centered experience mode in which the unit of experience is self-in-interaction-with-the-environment. However, with the transition out of narcissism and the subsequent differentiation processes this event-centered experience can occur on increasingly mature levels. The second is provisionally called a category-centered mode. It first becomes possible as a result of the transition out of narcissism. It is an organization of self aspects (and aspects of the environment), previously embedded in discrete events, into an increasingly comprehensive whole that cuts across events, and is organized according to the categories of consensually validated reality.

To refer to this as a bimodal identity organization implies that both modes are essential aspects of mature identity organization. The event-centered mode is not a primitive one normally supplanted by the "realistic" category-centered one. Rather, both are hypothesized to occur, optimally, on equally high levels of sophistication. The event-centered mode is centrally represented in the sense of self interacting with the environment. The category-centered one is experienced in the sense of self in terms of the general, as one among many to whom the same rules apply. In mature functioning these modes of identity experience interact with one another, each modifying and enriching the expression of the other.

Event-centered Post-narcissistic Identity Experience

The event-centered mode, perhaps the one always felt to be most essentially the core of self, is the product of differentiation of self and not-self out of narcissistic experiencing. Its outcome is a sense of self as thinker and center of will in productive relation to an impersonally functioning reality recognized as independent of self. (Self as separate person in relation to others, and of a particular sex in relation to other-sex persons are special cases of this general process.) The model of differentiation processes previously applied to children's achievement of a firm sense of themselves as boy or girl (see Chapters 2 and 3) appears to apply to identity development generally as well. After the developments of the narcissistic period and the narcissistic loss reactions, the differentiation processes proper begin. Both the self characteristics and those recognized as independent of self are differentiation products. Each is cognitively elaborated in distinctive ways. Each has a valid place in experience. Their development is complementary and inter-active. In optimal outcome narcissistic "experiencing" is replaced by an object relation: self in productive relation to what is independent of self and recognized to be so.

These differentiation processes occur centrally in developments out of primary creativity and of omnipotence, the two components of narcissistic experiencing. Differentiation out of the narcissistic illusion of primary creativity results in the sense of identity as thinker in relation to the objects of thought (consensually validated reality) recognized to be independent of self. The psychoanalytic literature generally refers to the relevant developments as the establishment of the worlds of imagination and perception, of the subjective and the objective, of the inner and the outer reality. The first is loosely identified with self, narcissism, primary process thought, and the pleasure ego, the second with external reality, reality testing, and secondary process thought. Frustrations imposed by reality result in the developments out of narcissism in which the first gives way to the second.

The differentiation perspective poses the problem differently. It suggests that in narcissistic "experiencing" it is cognition and the referents of cognition (that which is thought about) which are initially undifferentiated. Differentiation is not between an inner reality experienced as self and governed by primary process thought, and an intrusive outer reality governed by natural law, subject to rational thought, and so on. It is a differentiation out of one's global event-centered experiencing in which thought and physical actuality are not differentiated, into event-centered experience in which they are. One differentiation product is cognition (not only fantasy or primatively organized thought, but all thought). The other is a stable consensually validated reality. Cognition is identified with self; the consensually validated reality is recognized to be independent of self (i.e., of one's experiencing it either in fantasy or in rational thought). In optimal development both are accepted as valid aspects of experience. Thought is not felt to be ephemeral, "mere imagination" or inferior to "real facts." The consensually validated reality is neither felt to be the only "real" reality nor experienced as drab or bleak, "the dead hand of fact." Each is developed in distinctive ways. Thought is elaborated in the infinite complexities of perception, imagination, fantasy, memory, hypothesis, logic, and so forth. Knowledge of the consensually validated reality is elaborated in terms of the parameters of physical reality, social organization, and so on, recognized to exist independently of oneself. Reality is not seen as encroaching and diminishing self. Rather, self as thinker functions in interaction with reality independent of self in every action. This is obvious in perception and in memory, but even the wildest fantasy or dream is not a product of an inner life untouched by reality.

In optimum outcome, event-centered identity experience dominated by narcissistic processes gives way to event-centered identity experience in which self and that which is independent of self are fully differentiated. Now, within event-centered eperience, self as thinker functions in productive relation to a consensually validated reality recognized to be independent of one's perceptions, theories, or creative organizations of it. Regression is not a return to a highly cathected inner subjective world of imagination. It is a dedifferentiation of event-centered identity experience in which cognition and actuality are again subjectively fused or confused. In psychosis such fusion occurs in hallucination and delusion. In less profound regression it may be observed, for example, when, in anticipation of a probable event, an illusory conviction occurs instead of a sense of probability. Such unrealistic convictions can often be inferred only when the anticipated outcome does not occur and the individual's reaction is not one of disappointment but of a lost reality, of "the rug pulled out from under me," basically a feeling of threat to identity.

The second differentiation out of narcissistic, event-centered experience is a differentiation of the sense of omnipotence into a sense of self as center of will or intention in effective relation to events governed by physical causality. In Freud's conception the narcissistic sense of the omnipotence of wish is gradually given up in the face of frustrating reality. In regression the belief in the wish as arbiter of reality re-emerges.

The proposed framework does not posit an initial narcissistic belief that one's wishes (cognitions) are omnipotent. Rather, in narcissistic event-centered experience cognition (wishes or intentions) and the actualities to which they refer are undifferentiated. Both are aspects of the (as yet inchoate) self experience. Out of this undifferentiated event-centered experience both a sense of oneself as center of will (intention, wish) and a recognition of events governed by impersonal causality are differentiated. Both have valid places in experience. Self is not identified with narcissism, immaturity, and notions of omnipotence. Rather, self as center of will is elaborated in capacities for planning, skill development, instrumental action, and so forth. Events governed by physical causality are normally not perceived as predominantly frustrating factors inflicted from outside the self. In the prior narcissistic experiencing they have been part of the undifferentiated self experience. Recognition of them as independent of self is hypothesized to be the result of differentiation rather than of attention to a new arena of experience. Observation suggests that the parameters of such events (e.g., number, length, volume) are foci of curiosity rather than frustration. (The sense of them as frustrating impositions on the self is hypothesized to be an aspect of narcissistic loss reactions.) Intention and causality are elaborated in relation to one another, rather than the one being encroached on by the other. Their interaction as well as the importance of recognizing their independence is evident in every facet of the individual's intention, plan, or wish concerning the independent world.

The optimum outcome is not a sense of an omnipotent self shackled by the constraints of a frustrating reality. (Such an organization, in fact, would be seen as a failure of the differentiation processes.) It is event-centered identity experience in which a sense of self as center of will occurs in productive relation to events recognized to be independent of self. Regression is not a retreat from external reality to an internal, subjective world in which the wish is omnipotent. It is a return to an old mode of understanding one's interaction with the environment in which the narcissistic sense that all existence is a function of one's experiencing replaces the post-narcissistic object relationship.

The result of these differentiations out of primary creativity and omnipotence is an identity organization of self as center of thought and will in relation to a world independent of self. It is experienced in the event-centered mode. As a result of the differentiation processes (and the concurrent cross-event integration of event components to be discussed next) event-centered experience can occur on a post-narcissistic level (i.e., with full recognition of that which is independent of self). It is identity experience in the context of the particular, of self in relation to others, and to the non-human environment. In it self is central, not as creator of existence, but as organizer of experience (e.g., in perception, the imaginative organization of events, the elaboration of hypotheses, strategy planning). Within particular events aspects of others and of the non-human environment are adduced as they are relevant to self. Now, however, the aspects made focal in a particular event are increasingly recognized as parts of integrated wholes, rather than being part objects. Regression or incomplete development can be observed in narcissistic failure to take into account what is self and what is independent of self within event-centered experience.

In summary, this paradigm proposes that one aspect of the bimodal nature of mature identity organization is identity experience in the event-centered mode. It develops by differentiation out of the narcissistic sense of self as arbiter of all existence to a post-narcissistic recognition of what is self and what is independent of self. The two aspects of narcissism, the illusions of primary creativity and omnipotence are differentiated into self as thinker in relation to the objects of thought and self as center of will in relation to events determined by natural law. This form of identity experience is autocentric. It is experience of self in the particular. The organizing planful self is central and functions in effective relation to the human and non-human environment recognized as independent of self.

Category-centered Identity Experience

The second identity mode becomes possible when the capacity for symbolic thought permits the organization of event components (part objects) into whole objects. With the integration of self aspects across events, self becomes a self-aware, relatively coherent whole. Intrapsychic conflict can occur and repression replaces splitting in failed conflict resolution. The increasingly organized experience of the external world becomes the standard for reality, even for the reality of self aspects, and self becomes organized along the dimensions of consensually validated reality.

Self is experienced as central in new ways. It is no longer sensed to be arbiter of all existence. In fact, its own reality is tested against a standard outside itself, and it must recognize itself as one among many to whom the same rules apply. However, rather than consisting in an array of unintegrated self aspets, self is increasingly an integrated coherent unity. Although consensually validated reality is the final standard for the reality of self aspects, the existing self structure also functions as arbiter of the inclusion or exclusion of self aspects on the basis of their congruence with existing structures. Rather than self as a relatively undifferentiated aspect of an event, self can now stand apart, engaged in various events but wholly embedded in none, and the *sense* of identity increasingly inheres in the self structure rather than the event. Finally, self achieves new complexity and uniqueness as it integrates new categories (or new positions in old categories) into self (e.g., the man who is husband and becomes father has added a new category to his personality, but he is also different *as husband*. The daughter who becomes mother not only adds a new. category to her identity but modifies her sense of self as daughter as well).

Indications of Incomplete Dimension-Centered
Identity Organization in Borderline Disorders

In individuals with borderline and allied disorders phenomena occur that appear to reflect the incomplete or disturbed development of the second aspect of the bimodal identity organization. The incomplete development of a sense of self as a unity that participates in a variety of experiences seems often to be evident. For example, the severely disturbed Gary's experience of self-in-car-going-home-with-parents could not modulate the desolation of his sense of self-without-parents'-visit, though the preferred one was to substitute for the other at the identical time. Rather than an independent self that could feel united with parents *either* in the car going home *or* in a visit at the hospital the two self experiences remained independent of one another. Similarly, Deutsch's as-if painter patient seemed not to experience herself as a coherent unity involved in two quite different modes of artistic creation. Rather she seemed totally immersed, first in one self-in-interaction-with-the-environment constellation, then in the other.

When the sense of identity remains, to a significant extent, inherent in the event in which the individual is engaged rather than in the self independent of the particular event, difficulties may occur in transitions from one activity to another. In such a case a child may be unable to imagine himself in successive activities (at breakfast, on the way to school, in class, etc.) but finds himself successively in three discrete identity constellations and threatened with identity loss with the termination of each. This problem is not limited to children. Adults with borderline personality organizations may, for example, have significant difficulty in the transition from office to home. The office-centered identity and the home-centered one may be experienced as different personas. Memories (and experience generally) organized in the one may be relatively unavailable in the other, and the daily transition from one to the other and back again may be negotiated with difficulty, a quality of unease (or ceremonial organization) that is at bottom an experience of threat to identity.

When the self has not been thoroughly subject to the processes by which a coherent self is forged out of discrete and often incompatible self aspects, the individual's experience may be vivid and intense but shallow. Deutsch, for instance, describes her painter patient as initially very highly thought of by her successive teachers. Her assumption of their artistic modes was a complex identification, not just the adoption of a technique. However, she was unable to integrate the two differing styles into a personal style unique to herself. The richness of self experience that would have resulted from such integration was missing and her personality gradually impressed others as curiously empty.

In such persons a wide range of interests and commitments has had different meanings than a similarly wide range in persons whose self structure is more completely organized into a coherent whole. Individuals with borderline personality organizations are often observed to have a large number of discrete involvements. One of Deutsch's patients (1942), for example, was successively a member of the underworld, of a pietistic sect, of an artistic group, and of a political movement. Members of a nonclinical group hypothesized to have the same personality structure (Fast, 1974) had a continuing feeling of unlimited possibilities for themselves for example, "from circus clown to oceanographer, to duchess, to spy," and a multiplicity of identities could be shown in their actual professions and in the content of their dreams. However, if each of these dimensions of interest occurs relatively independent of one another the effect is different than if the integration process has occurred. In the latter case, for example, a member of a pietistic sect who has been a member of the underworld is different *as a member of the religious group* than one who has not. A duchess who is also an oceanographer is a different *duchess* than one who is not. A circus clown is a different clown if he is also a spy.

Correspondingly, the speed with which new characteristics can become part of oneself is different when integration into a coherent self structure is part of the process than when it is not. The teachers of Deutsch's painter patient were amazed at the rapidity with which she absorbed their artistic styles. Khan, similarly, speaks of the rapidity with which a schizoid patient may accept an interpretation, perceive its implications and express them in behavior, attitudes, and affective orientations. Members of the nonclinical group were often described as "quick studies," inordinately adept at the rapid acquisition of skills such as sailing, professional styles, languages, and so forth.

In such organizations, however, the new constellations leave the old ones (the other artistic orientation, the prior neurotic pattern) untouched. The time-consuming processes in which every aspect of the new orientation is integrated with every relevant aspect of the established organization of self (in clinical work, "working through") has not occurred.

Finally, from a developmental perspective, it is the integration of self across event-centered units that makes children's entry into the complexities of the oedipal period possible. When that development is incomplete or disturbed, as in individuals with borderline character organizations, discrete constellations of disparate or incompatible relationships with mothers and fathers may be elaborated. Integration of self aspects across constellations, however, requires the reconciliation of discrepancies. Self as boy cannot be integrated with representations of self as girl. Self as girl cannot be integrated with self in cross-sex relation to mother. Self as male living alone with mother is not compatible with self at home with beloved father and mother. Clinical work focused on oedipal issues with adults in whom the integration process is incomplete may not predominantly concern the resolution of neurotic solutions to oedipal problems, but more primitive issues. The oedipal issues may have been posed in only a rudimentary or fragmentary way. Their various elements may be presented in vivid form but in relatively discrete constellations whose incompatibility raises little intrapsychic conflict. The clinical problem, then, is to extablish the objectively incompatible self aspects as foci of intrapsychic conflict. It is only then that the resolution of those conflicts can become the central clinical issue.

Event- and Category-Centered Identity Experiences

The event-centered and the category-centered modes of identity experience are hypothesized to constitute a bimodal identity organization typical of maturity. These modes cannot be equated with notions still predominant in psychoanalytic psychology of an inner and an outer world, the subjective and objective, fantasy and reality, narcissistic and object related, the developmentally primitive and the developmentally mature.

Instead, they are viewed as representing two faces of mature identity experience, an autocentric and an allocentric one. One is experience in the particular, the other experience of self in terms of the general. One is a sense of self as center of thought and will. The other is self subordinated to an objective system of categories. One is self as center of experience. The other, self as one among many. One is likely to have easier access to emotion, intuition, the evocation of particular events. The other is more congruent with experience in terms of the general: rational analysis, hypothetico-deductive reasoning, and so forth. The expression of an idea in one context may more readily occur by metaphor, poetry, or drama, and in the other by prose and the orderly presentation of argument.

The event-centered mode predominates in the narcissistic period, and the category-centered one becomes possible only with the capacity for symbolic thought. However, the event-centered mode of identity experience is not replaced by the category-centered one. With the capacity for symbolic thought the event-centered one is gradually divested of its primitive narcissism and in mature identity experience both modes occur. Neither can validly be thought of as in its nature more mature than the other. Event-centered thinking may occur in primitive hallucinatory experience but also in poetic imagery at the highest levels of sophistication and subtlety. Similarly, category-centered thinking can occur on both primitive and sophisticated levels. Both modes are hypothesized to be required for optimal functioning in any activity, though in a particular event one or the other may predominate. Drama, for example, may represent the epitome of sophisticated event-centered organization. It represents the crystallization of a single event or idea. Within the play the protagonist is central and only those aspects of others and of the non-human environment that are relevant to the actualization of the protagonist's experience are included. Nevertheless, in the play's every aspect category-centered thought is implicated. Every component of the play (gesture, voice quality, language, clothing, social relationships, the non-human environment) must reflect accurate placement in the relevant categories of the historical, geographical, and cultural circumstances in which the play occurs. Conversely, in activity strongly dominated by the category-centered mode, such as theory building, there is a marked influence of the event-centered mode, expressed for example in intuition as to which of a number of lines of argument is most profitably pursued or in a steady awareness of the implications of a direction of theoretical elaboration for experience in the particular to which it will be applied

SUMMARY

Foundations for the development of identity are hypothesized to be established in the period of primary narcissism. In that period children's experience objectively occurs in adaptive interaction with the environment. Subjectively, however, because thought is not yet differentiated from its referents, illusions of omnipotence (that subjective experience is accompanied by the relevant actualities) and primary creativity (that events exist only as a function of one's experiencing them) prevail. Experience (e.g., nursing, grasping) is cognitively organized in relatively discrete units (events) composed of a self aspect interacting with aspects of the environment. Self is central (though without a sense of self). The infant's experiencing brings events into existence, and it is the activity of the self that determines which aspects of the environment are accorded a place in reality. Residues of this pattern of identity organization can be observed in borderline disorders.

At about age two a new identity organization becomes possible. The increasing differentiation of thought from its referents makes the transition out of narcissism possible. The capacity for thought in the absence of the objects of thought (i.e., symbolic thought) and the concurrent recognition of an environment independent on one's experiencing render the illusions of omnipotence and primary creativity untenable. They make intrapsychic conflict and reality testing possible and permit the organization of event components (self aspects, aspects of others and of the non-human environment) into wholes that cut across events and are tested against the categories of consensually validated reality. A bimodal identity organization results. One face of identity occurs in event-centered experience now divested of its narcissistic illusions. It is a sense of self as center of thought and will. The other, category-centered, is a sense of self in the context of the categories of consensual reality. The first is autocentric. It is experience in the particular with easier access to emotion, intuition, thought in terms of metaphor, poetry, or drama. The second is allocentric. It is experience in terms of the general, more closely associated with rational analysis and orderly presentation of argument. Both can occur at high levels of sophistication and both play a part in all activity of adulthood.

This paradigm for understanding identity structure and development is based on and broadly congruent with Freud's formulations of narcissism and transitions out of it. It hypothesizes a self ("das Ich," translated as self in Freud's early writing and variously as self or ego in later formulations) originating in an infantile narcissistic period in which self is centered in the infant's experience. It proposes, as Freud did, that major developments begin to occur at about age two, and that these can be understood as transitions out of narcissism. They include changes from narcissism to object relatedness, major changes in cognitive organization, and a new orientation to reality external to the self.

In significant ways, however, within these broad outlines the proposed model differs from Freud's and encourages different notions about identity. It suggests that narcissism is centrally a mode of understanding one's experience rather than an inward focus on the bodily self or the mother-child unit. Therefore the narcissistic identity organization is hypothesized to be a sense of self as arbiter of all existence (with its component illusions of omnipotence and primary creativity) rather than a "body ego." The infant's experience is conceptualized to occur from the beginning in increasingly efficient interaction with the environment, rather than centered on the body interior (or the mother-child unit) without cathexis of the environment. The narcissistic identity experience is not hypothesized to focus on the body self but on the individual's interactions with the environment *understood* narcissistically. The illusions of omnipotence and primary creativity are hypothesized to be the inevitable consequences of infantile experience in which cognition and actuality are not differentiated. Therefore, illusions of omnipotence and primary creativity are not notions that one's thoughts or wishes can affect reality. They are experiences in which thought and what is thought about are subjectively undifferentiated. The unit of experience is hypothesized to be the self-in-interaction-with-the-environment, not self focused on its own bodily experience. Therefore, the narcissistic sense of identity is hypothesized to reside in the event as a whole, not the self per se. The self-in-interaction-with-environment units are relationships among part objects. Therefore, primative identifications are not self aspects only but more similar to the dyads that Kernbeurg proposes.

The transition out of narcissism is not seen to be a consequence of a new cathexis of the external world but a change in the understanding of experience. Therefore, rather than a new interest in a previously uncathected external world, the transition is seen to result in a new *understanding* of well-established interactions with the environment. The change to object relatedness is not the result of a new interest in objects but a subjective recognition that interactions with the environment objectively present since birth are relationships to other persons and the non-human environment independent of self. It is a change from part object relationships embedded in relatively discrete events, to self and the human and non-human environment increasingly perceived as wholes and no longer bound to particular events. The cognitive change is hypothesized to be one from experience in which thought and the referents of thought are undifferentiated to experience in which thought can occur independently of its referents (i.e., symbolic thought) and the referents of thought are recognized to be independent of self. Therefore, the cognitive change in the transition out of narcissism is not hypothesized to be one from primary to secondary process thought, but the achievement of the capacity for symbolic thought and the consequent recognition that the illusions of omnipotence and primary creativity are untenable. Reality testing is not seen to be consequent on a new interest in the external world. Rather, the capacity for symbolic thought makes intrapsychic conflict possible. Conflict resolution can occur by appeal to a consensually validated reality (the external world) and in failed resolution, repression can replace splitting.

REFERENCES

Deutsch, H. (1942). Some forms of emotional disturbance and their relationships to schizophrenia. *Psychoanal. O.,*11: 301–321.

Deutsch, H. (1955). The impostor. *Psychoanal. O.,* 24: 483–505.

Fast, I. & Chethik, M. (1972). Some aspects of object relationships in borderline children. *Int. J. Psychoanal.,* 53: 479–485.

Fast, I. (1974). Multiple identities in borderline personality organization. *British J. Medical Psychol.,* 47: 291–300.

Fast, I. & Chethik, M. (1976). Aspects of depersonalization-derealization in the experience of children. *Int. J. Psychoanal.,* 3: 483–490.

Freud, S. (1911). Formulations on the two principles of mental functioning. *S.E.,* 12: 215.

Freud, S. (1914). On narcissism: An introduction. *S.E.,* 14: 69–81.

Freud, S. (1925). Negation. *S.E.,* 19:235.

Freud, S. (1925). Negation. S.E., 235-239.

Greenacre, P. (1958). The impostor. *Psychoanal. Q.*, 27:359-382.

Kernberg, O. (1966). Structural derivatives of object relationships. *Int. J. Psychoanal.*, 47: 236–253.

Khan, M. M. R. (1960). Clinical aspects of the schizoid personality: Affects and techniques. *Int. J. Psychoanal.*, 41: 430–437.

Piaget, J. (1951). Principal factors determining intellectual evolution from childhood to adult life. In D. Rappaport Ed. *Organization and Pathology of Thought,* New York: Columbia University Press.

Schafer, R. (1968). *Aspects of Internalization.* New York: International Universities Press.

Torok, M. (1970). The significance of penis envy in women. In Chasseguet-Smirgel Ed. *Female Sexuality: New Psychoanalytic Views,* Ann Arbor: University of Michigan Press.

6

Aspects of the Interplay of Masculinity and Femininity in Men and Women

Historical and cross-cultural evidence of human fascination with the interplay of male and female in the personality occurs in myth, art, and ritual. Plato reports a tale that traces the attraction of men and women for one another to their attempt to re-establish an original bisexual completeness that in the course of time had been separated into male and female parts. The myth of Hermaphrodite concerns the unification of lovers into a single being and the loss, by the creation of that absolute intimacy, of the capacity to love. The god Zeus functioned as a male in impregnating women but also himself gave birth to Athena. Sculptured figures with both male genitalia and breasts have been found among Eskimos[1] and in New Ireland (Otten, 1971, p. 224). Bettelheim (1954) discusses anthropological studies of male puberty rites in which cross-dressing, sub-incision, and other ceremonies explicitly or implicitly represent young men's assumption or relinquishing of female powers.

The academic and clinical traditions of psychological investigation have differed in the degree to which they have addressed the issues of this interplay. In academic psychology it has not been of significant interest. Studies of sexual social-

---

[1]Private collection.

ization, summarized in Maccoby and Jacklin's comprehensive work (1974), have tended to focus on the child's acquisition of gender-appropriate traits and preferences, and on parents' influences on gender-congruent socialization. A few studies concern parents' responses to gender-inappropriate behaviors in their sons and daughters but they do not deal with the interplay of masculinity and femininity within the child. Bem's (1974) concept of psychological androgyny contributes in that direction by raising the issue of the co-existence in the individual of masculinity and femininity. However, in its present operational form her notion of androgyny seems not to capture the intensity and complexity of meaning suggested in the cultural and clinical expressions. On the basis of logically independent, self-report scales of masculinity ("agentic" traits, e.g., to be ambitious, self-reliant) and femininity ("communal" traits, e.g., to be cheerful, sensitive to the needs of others) an individual is defined as masculine, feminine, or androgynous (high scores on both scales). Implicitly, to be androgynous is most desirable.

Is is otherwise in clinical investigation. The intra-individual interplay of masculinity and femininity is a commonplace of clinical practice and has been a longstanding focus of investigative interest, centrally within psychoanalytic psychology. The referents of the terms masculinity and femininity and notions of their interplay are different from those in Bem's work. The individual's own conceptions of what it is to be masculine and feminine are at issue. Masculinity and femininity are not observed to co-exist comfortably in the individual. Instead their interplay tends to occur in the context of disturbance in gender identity. The disturbance takes two basic forms. On one hand individuals accurately recognize that some characteristics are ruled out for them on the basis of their sex (e.g., child-bearing for men; male genitals for women), but are unable to relinquish those possibilities. (See Bettelheim (1954) and Kubie (1974) for extended discussions). On the other hand, individuals may have convictions (of which they may or may not be fully aware) that some characteristics (e.g., tenderness, mathematical talent, creativity, administrative capacity) are absolutely sex-linked and therefore aberrant in themselves and in conflict with their gender identities. Such notions may result in significant personal difficulty, for example, in father-child relations for men who find their nurturant impulses unacceptably feminine; or in work problems for women who identify competence with masculinity, or men who perceive creativity and productivity to be female and as absolutely denied them as child-bearing.

Within psychoanalytic psychology Freud's model and the gender differentiation perspective imply differing organizations of this interplay some of whose characteristics can be explored in individuals' interpretations of the ambiguous stimuli of the Rorschach inkblots. One of these is the persistence of bisexuality in adulthood. In Freud's developmental theory the boy is conceived of as being male and masculine in all respects from the time of birth, the girl as being initially male and masculine, and achieving femininity in the course of development. In this formulation women, having to overcome an initial masculinity to achieve femininity, may be expected to show greater evidence of bisexuality than men. In Freud's bisexuality theory male and female themes are posited to be present in both men and women from the beginning of life. There is no basis in this formulation for predicting a sex difference in the persistence of bisexuality. Therefore, Freud's models of gender development predict either a predominance of bisexual themes in women or no sex difference in such themes.

In contrast, the gender differentiation perspective proposes that bisexual themes normally occur in both boys and girls when they become aware of sex difference. However, because the mother tends to be the central caregiver in this society boys are likely to have more difficulty than girls in accepting the fact that femininity cannot be theirs (see Chapter 3 for extended discussion). This conception, thus, predicts greater prevalence of bisexual themes in men than in women.

The Hypothesis

The primary prediction of this study, therefore, was that, in response to the Rorschach inkblots men would more frequently than women report bisexual imagery. When this hypothesis proved to be supported by the data the Rorschach responses were explored for imagery that might give further indication of residues of difficulties with sex difference issues in men. The available data lent themselves particularly to some exploration of men's continuing reactions to women's capacities for child bearing as a sex difference issue.

METHOD

Subjects

The sample included all the adult patients to whom the Rorschach test was administered in one out-patient clinic in the 25 years of its existence.[3] The clinic serves the general community in a university town. Its orientation is toward intensive psychoanalytically-oriented psychotherapy. The occupational and educational range represented in the patient group, therefore, is likely to tend toward the middle class and well-educated. Within the patient population the subgroup to whom the Rorschach test was administered varied over the years with changes in clinic policy and availability of diagnostic services. It is probably safe to assume, however, that the group for whom Rorschach protocols were available included a preponderance of persons perceived to be relatively seriously disturbed because those were more likely to be engaged in the more extensive evaluation that involved Rorschach testing.

A total of 203 patient Rorschach protocols were available. Of the 203 patients 102 were men, 101 were women. The mean age of the men was 21.7, S.D. 10.1; of the women 24.2, S.D. 6.6.

Prodecures

Responses to Cards II and III of the Rorschach test were used to compare male and female patients' production of bisexual

---

[3] I am grateful to the Center for the Clinical Study of Personality for making the necessary clinical materials available to me and facilitating their use.

imagery. The Rorschach cards were used because they provide ambiguous stimuli in which individuals may see male or female figures, and in the case of some cards, they see bisexual ones. The protocols from this clinic were particularly useful because methods of administration, care in inquiry into the particulars of interpretations, and specificity and clarity of recording were of a high order. There was no reason to expect that what variability existed in this regard over the years would affect the protocols of males and of females differentially.

Cards II and III were selected as ones that clinical experience indicated readily elicited both male and female imagery, and might elicit bisexual imagery as well. On Card II (usual animals with paws together) Klopfer Area d1 is frequently seen as a penis. The adjacent interior white area and the red below (D1) are often seen as female internal genitals and menstrual blood. Bisexual imagery would involve a fusion of these male and female images in one interpretation. On Card III Klopfer Popular Area 1 is frequently interpreted as two human figures facing one another. Projections in the chest area are often viewed as breasts and the figures identified as female, and ones on the upper leg as penises and the figures identified as male. A bisexual interpretation would be one in which the figures were interpreted has having both breasts and penises.

Explicit coding criteria were developed only for coding bisexual imagery in response to Card III because no person explicitly included male and female imagery in a single percept in response to Card II. In establishing coding categories for responses to Card III it seemed advisable in this initial study to limit the scoring of Bisexuality to the most explicit and face-valid images. The following are the coding criteria.

Code I

Bisexuality

Explicit interpretation of the human (or anthropomorphized animal) figures as both male and female (e.g., "it has both

breasts and a penis"; "a man but with breasts"; "a woman and she seems to have the male part too").
Or
The subject refers to both maleness and femaleness in the interpretation but expresses puzzlement or doubt (e.g., "seems incongruous"; "kind of unlikely"). However S *does not* specify that the sexually differentiating characteristics of the figure would determine its sex differentially (e.g., S *does not* say "if these are breasts then it's a woman, if this is a penis it's a man"; or "could be either one, depending on whether you use the breast or the penis").

A more inclusive code (Sexual Ambiguity) was developed as well. In these reponses there was greater evidence of individuals' attempts to resolve the bisexual interpretation than was permitted in the Bisexuality score, but resolution of the bisexuality issue remained incomplete.

Code 2

Sexual Ambiguity

The subject shows additional critical capacity. S specifies that if the figure is one of sex it cannot stimultaneously be of the other sex and or have sex-specific characteristics of the other sex (e.g., S *does* make the statements he (she) *does not* make in the second Bisexuality category (e.g., "If this is a breast it's a woman, if this is a penis, it's a man")). However, S *does not resolve* the ambiguity in an interpretation of the figure as male or as female (e.g., *does not* say, "Ignoring this part (usual penis), it's a woman"; or I'll make them men in tuxedos. This (usual breasts) can be shirts with ruffles.").

Satisfactory inter-rater reliability was established. Because bisexuality was expected to occur relatively rarely, reliability established using a randomly selected group of protocols was likely to be spuriously high. Therefore a group of 26 protocols was constituted of 10 males and 10 female cases with consecutive file numbers, coded by one rater as neither

Bisexual or Sexually Ambiguous, plus 4 consecutively num-
bered cases coded Bisexual and 2 coded Sexually Ambiguous.
These were coded by the second rater. The percent agreement
was 95, the raters having disagreed in the coding of one case.

RESULTS AND DISCUSSION

The sex ratio of the frequency of responses coded Bisexual and
Sexually Ambiguous supports the Gender Differentiation
framework rather than Freud's formulations. The gender differentiation hypothesis predicted that bisexual imagery
would occur more frequently among men than among women.
In reponse to the ambiguous stimulus of Rorschach Card III,
and using the restrictive Bisexual Coding, 13 of 203 individuals responded with bisexual imagery. Of these 11 of 102
were men, 2 of 101 were women (d.f. $1, x^2$ 6.57, p. .02). The
more inclusive Sexually Ambiguous coding added an additional 6 to the 11 cases coded Bisexual. Of these 5 were men, 1
was a woman. Using the more inclusive coding (summing
Bisexual and Sexually Ambiguous responses), 16 of 102 men
and 3 of 101 women reported sexually ambiguous imagery
(d.f. 1, x^2 9.67, p. .005).[4]
    The character of the reponses coded Bisexual and Sexually
Ambiguous support views prevalent in clinical investigation
(but contrary to Bem's notions of psychological androgyny)
that the internal co-existence of masculinity and femininity is
disturbing to the individual and that the disturbance concerns gender identity. Examples of men's and women's interpretations of Rorschach Card III coded Bisexual:

"(Male) These are two people—strange. They seem to look sort
of like women actually, but the heads don't at all. The bodies at

---

[4]David Diamond has successfully replicated these findings in a
study using a sample of patients hospitalized for psychiatric reasons
and therefore probably more seriously disturbed than the patients
in the present sample (Diamond, D. J., Problems in Gender Identity.
unpublished paper, University of Michigan, 1979).

any rate do . . . This protrusion makes me think of an erect penis on the leg except that it's coming out of the knee rather than way up where it ought to be."

"(Male) A ritual dance or sacrifice . . . blood sacrifice. Aboriginal figures . . . Breast and penis . . . seasonal mythology . . . very homosexual in the sense of being female and male . . . sexual confusion here."

"(Male)" Two guys. Two jungle natives with big breasts and high heels on. Beating on bongos. Sex organs hanging out. (Inq.) Male—big breasted. In Africa, where males have big breasts also."

"(Female) Two women carrying something . . . Bisexual figures. Women having both breasts and penis."

Examples of interpretations coded Sexually Ambiguous:

"(Male) These could be dancing figures except both are male or on the other hand the projection here could be breasts. Dancing or ice skating. Below could be a shadow . . . if I make them both ghostly figures rising out of darkness . . . red seems to be coming between them . . . watching or controlling them as they go through the predetermined movements of the dance."

"(Male) To me this is two women except it looks like they have penises—pulling ribs (Klopfer Area D3). (Inq.) Looks as if they both had large breasts and also on their feet shoes with large heels. It could have gone either way . . . two things outbalance the one . . . a rib cage . . . a man's rib cage . . . a skeleton. I say man's, could have been a woman's, a human rib cage."

"(Female) This is two men facing each other . . . The reason I said men is the shape of their hands and legs. Then they had female attributes but somehow too, they were more like men (Inq.) . . . Then I thought they might be women because they have breasts. But I don't associate skinny legs with women . . ."

Freud's hypothesis (gender development theory) that boys typically attribute male genitals to women to avoid recognition of sex differences (see Chapter 3) does not, strictly speaking, lead to the prediction that men are likely to report such bisexual images as women with both female and male attributes. Nonetheless the clinical literature seems to suggest that the notion of the "phallic mother" may be a bisexual one. If such notions determined the greater frequency of bisexual imagery in men it might be expected that men's bisexual images would be predominantly of women with penises, rather than either of men with breasts or of androgynous figures. Such a possibility was not supported in these data. Of the 11 Bisexual images reported by men three were female (witches, a couple of women, two people . . look like women), two were male (butlers, two guys . . . jungle natives), and six were not identitied as of one sex or the other (hermaphrodites, neonphindites (sic), aboriginal figures (2), African fetish symbols, people).

A number of other factors that might render the obtained results spurious were considered and could be discounted. The total group was almost equally divided between men and women (102:101). No significant sex difference occurred in subjects' use of the figures on Card III as human (Male: Female, 84:81). Of these, 50 men and 54 women assigned a specific sex to the figures (exclusive of those coded Bisexual or Sexually Ambiguous). The possibility that men described more bisexual imagery than women because they were more willing to speak of specifically sexual matters was checked by comparing the number of male and female subjects who used genital imagery on Card II only (in order not to confound this comparison with comparisons of bisexual imagery on Card III). The male-female ratio (27:22) indicated somewhat greater male articulation of sexual imagery, but not approaching satistical significance or sufficient to account for the 11:2 male-female ratio of Bisexual imagery and the 5:1 ratio of Sexually Ambiguous imagery on Rorschach Card III.

The statistically significant predominance of bisexual imagery in men suggested a search for other indicators of male difficulty in the resolution of gender differentiation issues, specifically in relation to giving up the possibilities of child-bearing. The interior white space of Rorschach Card II frequently evokes imagery of the pelvis, womb, or abdomen. If gender differentiation hypotheses are valid, this inkblot area might be expected to stimulate imagery in men reflecting feelings of loss or damage to themselves in that bodily area, destructive wishes toward females, indicators of developmentally early notions of child-bearing as an anal activity, and/or confusion of male and female genital function or anatomy (though less explicit than that which could have been coded Bisexual or Sexually Ambiguous). Because relinquishing the capacity for child-bearing is hypothesized to be a sex difference issue for men but not for women, similar imagery would not be expected to occur in women.

Ten men and eleven women reported pelvic or abdominal imagery in response to the interior white area of Rorschach Card II. Themes congruent with gender differentiation theory were prominent in men's imagery.

Approximately half the men, but no women, reported imagery involving themes of loss or damage. In some cases it referred clearly to feelings of damage to the man. Examples:

> "(in reverse position) A genital area of a male . . . penis, prostrate (sic) hanging down. The white central portion seems to be the rectum, anus, as far as I can see. Also seems to be a purely geometric form . . . hollow or concave, and a hole at the bottom of it . . . a surrealistic painting of human anatomy. (Inq.) . . . generally looks like a man that's disembowelled, . . . torn, with his genitals remaining intact . . . whole thing, as if something had been scooped out and someone had punched a hole in it . . . extreme distortion . . . symbolic."

> "(reverse position) This looks like a penis . . . two testicles here, as though they're smashed or something . . . they're bleeding. This (center white) would also be an abdomen here with a big hole in it . . . a cannonball has gone through. (Inq.) It (the abdomen) was right above the penis."

In one case the imagery was of deliberate damage to the woman, specifically in relation to her child-bearing capacity:

"A female sex organ . . . I once watched a delivery . . . (Inq.) If you've ever seen a woman garotted (sic) for delivery . . . . The whole groin area: vagina, anus, clitoris, urethral opening . . . terror of pictures . . . about conflict and child-birth associated with pain."

Seven of the ten men, but no women, reported imagery that included references to the lower intestine or anus. In the first example above, the anal imagery occurs in the context of damage to the male body. In another, notions of anus and vagina appear to be confused in relation to a sense of something missing in the abdomen:

"A hole through something . . . inflamed tissue around some anal or vaginal orifice. (Inq.) Just seems to be a hole through something. An emptiness through a substance. In some way it doesn't please me. I wouldn't leave it there if I were going to fix it . . . in general it looks vaguely vaginal . . . I don't know what anal disease produces an inflamation."

In still another, anal imagery occurs with a focus on the "abnormally large" size of female genitalia:

"(Card in reverse position) At least two possible interpretations . . . As genitalia . . . in the case of the male it would be a very short penis. In the case of the woman there is a brief crack, a slit which could be a vagina . . . There is also a dark slit which could be the anus . . . Then you have an abnormally large vaginal cavity."

Finally, in one case the fusion of male and female was explicit though the patient had sufficient critical judgment to recognize it and suggest that two views were represented:

"A man's rear end or his ass. (Inq.) Between the legs . . . two banks with a passage in the middle . . . two crevices and a ravine in the middle, and blood like a woman's period . . . first assume it would be a woman, but then switch over to a man. Don't know why."

The imagery reported by the eleven women who reported abdominal or pelvic interpretations was distinctly different. No women reported imagery suggesting feelings of loss in the self or wish to damage, (though in one case the notion of menstrual blood implied the possibility of a wound, (see below)). In no case was anal imagery reported. There were no images of sexual confusion.

Women's abdominal imagery in all eleven cases concerned the female pelvic area. In three cases it seemed subsidiary to a focus on the lower red as menstrual blood. Example:

> "Blood . . . from a wound. Pelvis, the hole in the middle. (Inq.) could be menstrual blood . . . but I don't think of blood spurting from that area."

The remaining eight responses explicitly concerned childbearing. Examples:

> "X-ray of part of a woman . . . bearing of child. (Inq.) Not a child in here . . ."

> "Pelvic bone . . . birth processes. (Inq.) I saw diagrams of pregnancy. I only had my baby recently."

Taken together, the statistically significant male-female differences in Bisexual and Sexually Ambiguous imagery and the sex differences in imagery response to Rorschach Card II support gender differentiation hypotheses accounting for the intra-individual interplay of masculinity and femininity. The study's results are contrary to significant aspects of Freud's gender development theory, specifically that boys are unequivocally masculine, that they are concerned only about damage to their penises, that the child-bearing capacities of women are of no dynamic concern to them, and that bisexual themes are likely to be more prominent in women than in men. The results are neither contrary to nor supportive of Freud's notion of a constitutional bisexuality in both men and women, except as they support the notions of a developmental origin for bisexuality.

The postulates of gender differentiation theory concerning the interplay of masculinity and femininity in the personality are supported. Patients' reported imagery suggests that the intra-individual interplay of masculinity and feminity can be observed in adults. When it occurs, at least in this patient group, it appears to be associated with anxiety and conflict. The conflict seems to have to do with unresolved issues of sex difference. It appears to concern difficulty in accepting the limits imposed by one's actual sex. In the form explored in this study it occurs more frequently in men than in women. For some men, women's child-bearing capacity appears to be of continuing significant concern in adulthood. Their reported imagery suggests feelings of loss or destruction in relation to it, destructive wishes toward women's child-bearing body parts, the retention of an anal model of child-birth rather than replacement by recognition of female anatomy and functions, and the persistence of a confusion of male and female sexual anatomy.

SUMMARY

The intra-individual interplay of masculinity and femininity is a commonplace of clinical work though it has not been extensively explored in academic psychology. Freud's formulations of gender development and of bisexuality have provided the predominant paradigms for understanding it. The gender differentiation theory is shown to differ from Freud's model in its predictions concerning the intra-individual interplay of masculinity and femininity in adult men and women. Freud's views suggest no sex difference (bisexuality theory) or a greater frequency in women (gender development theory). Gender differentiation theory predicts a greater frequency in men. Predicted sex differences in bisexual imagery responsive to the ambiguous stimulus of Rorschach Card III support the gender differentiation hypothesis and imagery responsive to Rorschach Card II supports the theoretical premises from which the hypothesis was derived.

REFERENCES

Bem, (1974). The measurement of psychological androgeny. *J. of Cons. Cli. Psych.,* 42:155–162.

Bettelheim, B. (1954). *Symbolic Wounds.* New York: The Free Press.

Freud, S. (1905). Three essays on the theory of sexuality. *S.E.* Vol. VII, Hogarth Press.

Freud, S. (1918). From the history of an infantile neurosis. *S.E.* Vol. XVII, Hogarth Press.

Kubie, L. S. (1974). The drive to become both sexes. *Psychoanal. Q.,* 43:349–426.

Maccoby E. M. And Jacklin, C. N. (1974), *The Psychology of Sex Differences* Stanford University Press.

Otten, C. M. (1971). *Anthropology and Art.* Where published? The Natural History Press.

Stoller, R. J. (1968). *Sex and Gender.* Where published? Jason Aronson.

7

The Wolf Man: Some
Differentiation Perspectives

Freud's formulation of the dynamics of the "Wolf Man" centers on the complexities of a boy's reactions to the recognition of sex difference. Therefore, and because the case is well known to most people familiar with psychoanalytic literature, it provides a useful context in which to show how a differentiation paradigm might suggest additional or differing directions for exploration in a particular case.

It is hazardous to suggest alternative interpretations of clinical material already presented in a case study. Such an attempt has all the problems of working with secondary sources. The data are necessarily incomplete, selection for the intial presentation having been made from a larger universe of observation. The material has been selected for its contributory value to the particular themes being developed in that presentation. Data needed to test alternative hypotheses may not be included or may be included in a form not useful for the required analysis. Moreover, particularly salient to the analysis of clinical material, the possibility of testing hypotheses in ongoing clinical work is absent. However, the case material in this instance appears to be sufficiently extensive and the presentation broad enough in scope to warrant an attempt if it is limited to those themes for which the available supporting data are most convincing, and if it is understood that the alternative perspectives offered are to be taken only as illustrative of hypotheses that might be tested clinically in comparable circumstances.

The subject of Freud's discussion was a wealthy young Russian who began analysis with Freud in his mid-twenties. The case presentation, however, is a reconstruction of a phobia and subsequent obsessional neurosis that occured in the patient's childhood. The phobia focused on the picture of a wolf in a story book for children. In it the wolf was represented standing upright and striding along. Whenever the boy saw the picture he screamed wildly that the wolf was going to eat him up. The patient remembered the picture as illustrating the story either of Little Red Riding Hood or of The Wolf and the Seven Little Goats. (After many hours in bookstores during his analysis he was able to establish that the picture illustrated the story of The Wolf and the Seven Little Goats).

A dream heralded the onset of the phobia. It occurred on the eve of the boy's fourth birthday, which was also Christmas eve:

> I dreamt that it was night and that I was lying in my bed (My bed stood with its foot towards the window; in front of the window there was a row of old walnut trees. I know it was winter when I had the dream, and night-time). Suddenly the window opened of its own accord and I was terrified to see that some white wolves were sitting on the big walnut tree in front of the window. There were six or seven of them. The wolves were quite white and looked more like foxes or sheep dogs for they had big tails like foxes and they had their ears pricked like dogs when they pay attention to something. In great terror, evidently of being eaten up by the wolves, I screamed, and woke up (p. 29).[1]

Freud interpreted this anxiety dream and the subsequent phobia in terms of his developmental and bisexuality theories. They were, he suggested, the result of the boy's new

---

[1]Unless otherwise specified, page numbers refer to material as it occurs in the case study (Freud, 1918).

capacity for understanding a number of earlier events which at the time of their occurrence were not anxiety arousing. The earliest of these was his observation of his parents in sexual intercourse when he was a year and a half old. Analysis of the patient's memories and associations convinced Freud that in this event the father, standing, had entered the mother from behind. The patient, possibly due to an unusually strong feminine component in his constitutional bisexuality, identified with the mother's role in this situation, an identification that contributed to a later wish to be copulated with by his father. More recently, when he was just past three years of age he had been the passive partner in sexual activity with his sister who was two years older than he. At her instigation too, he played with his penis in the presence of his Nanya (nurse) who had warned him against it, saying that a "wound" might result. Since the seduction by his sister his sexual curiosity had become intense. Two issues were uppermost in his mind. One was the possibility that one could be without a penis. Among the associated memories was one of having watched his sister and another girl urinating. Another was a memory of his governess referring to a stick of candy as cut up snakes and of his father killing a snake with a stick. He had also wondered what it meant to call a horse a gelding. And he had heard a story about a wolf and a tailor in which the tailor pulled the tail off the fox, and another in which a fox lost his tail when he went fishing and used it for bait. The other focus of his sexual curiosity was the question of the origin of babies. He had found recent trips to a sheep breeding farm very exciting. Two fairy tales interested him particularly, the stories of Little Red Riding Hood and of The Wolf and the Seven Little Goats. A wolf occurred in each of these and in each live children were taken from the wolf's body. He wondered whether possibly this meant that the wolf was not male, or whether, perhaps, males could bear children too. He cherished the notion derived from his Nanya, that he was his father's child and his sister the child of his mother.

Until the time of the dream and phobia these various experiences had been occasions for curiosity rather than anxiety. Now, however, his cognitive development made it possible for him to recognize the implications of sex difference. Under the dominance of the feminine theme of his bisexuality he wished to take the female role in copulation with his father. He now realized, however, that if he were to actualize his feminine wishes he would lose his penis. Specifically, to be male is to have a penis. To be female is to have a wound or hole that results when the penis is removed. That is, he could be either male or castrated. The wish to actualize his feminine wishes was in conflict with his wish to retain his penis. A struggle ensued between his masculine and feminine tendencies. His masculinity was ego-syntonic. He made energetic efforts to repress his feminine tendencies. It was the conflict resulting from this wish to take the female role and his fear that to realize that wish meant castration that was expressed in the dream and phobia.

Freud summarizes the underlying meanings of the dream images as follows (p. 42, n. 2). The setting of the dream has the dreamer asleep in bed. The window opening by itself represents his wakening out of sleep to awareness of his parents in sexual intercourse. The big walnut tree represents a Christmas tree and anticipation of the pleasures of Christmas morning. It also refers to the tree in the story of the wolf and the tailor in which the wolf loses his tail, and thus to the possibility of castration, and perhaps to a wish to observe without being seen as one can do from a tree, and as a little boy might have done when observing his parents' sexual activity. The number of wolves (6 or 7) refers to the story of The Wolf and the Seven Little Goats in which the wolf eats six of seven kids. The central referent, the "two" of copulation, is disguised by this larger number. The wolves sitting in the tree represent the Christmas presents the boy hoped to receive on the following day. They also, by reversal, refer to the wolves in the tailor story who were under the tree, and therefore to castration. Another reversal is the wolves' immobility that represents its opposite, the agitated movements of the parents. The wolves' strained attention refers to the boy's intent observation of the parents' activity. The wolves' being white refers multiply to the bed clothes of the parents, white sheep the boy had seen on his visit to the sheep breeding farm, the whitened paw of the wolf as he attempted to fool the kids into thinking his paw was the hand of their mother, and trees at the boy's home that were once entirely covered with caterpillar tents. The wolves' big tails like foxes denies the possibility of castration. The boy's terror that he would be eaten up represents the underlying fear of castration and wakens him.

In Freud's view, these meanings of the dream images reflect two major themes. The superficial references in the dream are to Christmas. Underlying these, one major group of dream images refers in various ways to the parents in sexual intercourse. This imagery results from the boy's wish for sexual satisfaction from his father in which he would take the role of the mother. The other refers to the possibility of castration. It stems from the boy's new capacity to recognize the implications of sex difference, that if he were to actualize his sexual wish in relation to his father he would forfeit his penis. The anxiety is the product of the conflict between his wish and his fear.

This same conflict is represented in the phobia. The wolf's posture is that of the father in sexual intercourse with the mother, in which he entered her from behind. The boy's wish, an expression of his constitutionally based femininity, is to take the female role in such copulation with the father. His fear is that to do so means being castrated, to have a wound instead of a penis, to be female.

This highly condensed presentation of Freud's interpretation of the dream and phobia can be of service only to remind the reader already familiar with the case study of salient issues. In his further extensive presentation of the case Freud elaborates the relevant issues both as they appeared clinically and in terms of their theoretical significance.

In five areas Freud's case presentation appears to offer sufficient material to show how a differentiation perspective would invite clinical exploration in alternative or additional directions. The first four focus centrally on the proposition that on recognition of sex difference, this boy's conflicts were predominently about the femininity he must give up as a possibility for himself rather than about wishes to take a female role in copulation with his father. First, the differentiation framework would suggest that a significant aspect of the patient's struggles when he became able to recognize the implications of sex difference, concerned the recognition of limits, specifically a reluctance to give up the possibility of having unlimited sex and gender possibilities (i.e., bisexual completeness). Second, it would invite clinical focus on the mother's place in the patient's struggles with issues of sex difference. Third, it would suggest that the boy's preoccupation with giving birth and with the origin of babies concerned issues of sex difference. Fourth, it would invite attention to possible sex difference issues underlying his anal difficulties.

The fifth suggests a role for the father in the patient's gender development different than the one Freud proposes. The father is not seen only to be the powerful male with whom the boy wishes to take a female or male role. Rather, the differentiation model proposes that the father normally plays significant roles in the earliest establishment of self representations, in providing a focus for identification in the boy's struggles with issues of sex difference, and in being a figure for competitive rivalry and consolidation of gender identity in his oedipal struggles. It suggests that this father's illnesses and absences significantly interferred with his playing his appropriate role for the patient in the second and third of these phases.

The Wish for Bisexual Completeness

Differentiation theory suggests that one, normally transient, response of boys to the recognition of sex difference is the wish or illusion that they need not relinquish the possibility of bearing children. In this patient's dream and phobia as well as in related case material, there are indications that he was concerned with the notion of a male being bisexually complete. The central focus of his phobia was the pictured wolf. In Freud's view it was the wolf's posture, like that of the erect father in intercourse with the mother, that was central. The active, erect, intrusive father represented constitutionally based maleness. The boy's wish was to take the female role in relation to it. However, additional possibilities are suggested by the meanings the wolf picture had for the boy. The wolf that was the focus of his phobia was a very particular one. It was the wolf that illustrated either the story of Little Red Riding Hood or the Wolf and the Seven Little Goats. The stories were linked in the boy's mind by the similar role of the wolf in them. The patient's remembered concerns about whether the wolf in these stories might be female because live babies were taken from its body or whether, perhaps, males too could bear children, imply both that the boy knew that child-bearing was a female capacity and that there was something attractive to him in the notion that a male too might have it. That is, one theme underlying the phobia may have been as Freud suggests, a wish to take a female role in relation to the dominant, active, intrusive male one represented by the wolf. Another, however, appears to contribute strongly to the selection of this particular wolf image as the phobic object: the wish to be male but to have female capacities too.

In the dream that heralded the phobia, too, the wolf imagery appears to subsume notions of bisexual completeness. The number of wolves (six or seven) recalled to the dreamer the little goats the male wolf swallowed, which were later taken live out of his body. The character of the dream wolves themselves suggests bisexuality in two major ways. First, the wolves had faces like sheep dogs and large tails like foxes. Freud draws attention to the large tails as symbols of masculinity. Combined with the maternal connotations of sheep dogs, the image is one of a bisexually complete figure. Second, the wolves were white. Freud suggests a possible association to the white bedclothes in the incident of the parents' intercourse. The larger number of associations to the whiteness, however, refer to issues of giving birth. The story of the Wolf and the Seven Little Goats occurs again in the patient's associations: the white of the dream wolves is referred to the wolf in the story whitening his paw to impersonate the goat mother and secure access to the little goats. The white color reminded the patient too of his visits to a sheep breeding farm. In addition to the possibility that Freud suggests, that the boy may have seen sheep copulating, and the ram in a position reminiscent of the father in intercourse with the mother, images of a sheep breeding farm are likely to evoke notions of pregnant sheep or sheep with lambs. Finally, the wolves' white color reminded the patient of a time when trees at his home were covered with white caterpillar tents, constructions centrally involved with reproduction. That is, in the dream as well as the phobia the wolf, consistently seen as a male figure, is associated with imagery suggesting a wish that a boy, without giving up his maleness, could have the capacities and attributes of females as well.

Symptoms in the subsequent obsessional neurosis and in his later paranoid disorder also support the notion that issues of bisexual completeness may have been important for him. In the obsessional neurosis the question of who could give birth played a significant part. On the basis of his Nanya' statement that his sister was his mother's child and he his father's, he had maintained the belief that men as well as women could bear children. Now he became involved in obsessive ruminations about who had given birth to Christ. Joseph and Mary were Christ's parents, but Joseph was also described as only *like* a father to him. God was Christ's father. At the same time Mary was considered to be the Mother of God. The boy was unable to resolve the riddles involved, or perhaps, was unable to accept the facts of sex difference required for their resolution.

Finally, the paranoid episode in adulthood for which Brunswick treated him (Brunswick, 1928) began with a delusional preoccupation that suggests the recrudescence of bisexual imagery. In the context of intensifying narcissistic regression, the patient became obsessed with the possibility of a blemish on his nose. His nose had earlier been a focus of conflict about the adequacy of his masculinity. Now he perceived on it what he called "a hole, a crease, or a scar." Physicians and others whom he begged to look at it found the hole difficult or impossible to see. He himself, however, was obsessed with it. The notions of "a hole, a crease, or a scar" suggest fantasies of femaleness. His compulsive behavior in relation to it also did so. He incessantly looked at himself in a pocket mirror, ostensibly to see whether the hole had burgeoned, was still there, or had gone away, and he constantly powdered his nose, explicitly to hide what had become the focus of his fascinated attention. This occurrence of notions of the growth of female characteristics associated with his nose that was for him a symbol of his masculinity would suggest, in a differentiation paradigm, the possibility of a narcissistic dedifferentiation in the area of gender, and the reemergence of attractive and frightening images of himself as both male and female.

The occurence of bisexual themes underlying the wolf imagery in the dream and phobia, and suggestions of unresolved conflicts about the recognition of limits in the subsequent obsessional neurosis and the later paranoid episode do not invalidate Freud's analysis of the wolf imagery. An image may subsume a variety of themes. However, they do suggest a useful focus for clinical investigation might have been the patient's difficulties in recognizing limits in the area of sex and gender.

Envy of Females

In Freud's view the father was central in the boy's difficulties. He notes that the boy grew up in an almost exclusively female household and that his older sister was a particularly dominant and intrusive influence. However, in his interpretation of the clinical material he attributes the boy's feminine orientations almost exclusively to constitutionally determined wishes to take a passive female role in copulation with the male (his father). Similarly, Freud did not view the patient's later difficulties with his mother and sister, and with women generally, as specific to his ambivalence toward women themselves, but due to an underlying wish to receive from the man as the woman does.

The differentiation perspective would suggest that for the boy the mother is a significant focus of conflict in her own right when he becomes aware of sex difference and that these conflicts may shape his later relations to women. It would invite attention, therefore, to the possibility that this boy's feelings toward women might include envy, feelings that women have deprived him of something rightly his, and spiteful wishes to regain from them what he lacks.

The two fairy tales most closely linked to the phobia and the dream suggest such themes. In each the wolf is clearly male. In each he lurks near the female (the house of the mother goat, Little Red Riding Hood in the woods and at her grandmother's house), whose possessions are the object of his hungry fascination. His interest in the females and their possessions is not secondary to his involvement with males. It is the female herself who has what he wants. In each story he gets what he wants by stealing it from her. His resulting satisfaction is not in securing for himself what the woman has been given by the male, but in getting what he perceives to be the female's own.

The presented case material about the patient's actual relationships suggests, too, that women played a central part in his life, that they were major foci of conflict and that a significant theme in his difficulties with them concerned sex difference issues of envy, feelings that women had what he lacked and wishes to deprive them as he felt deprived by them. There are indications that within the context of his largely female surroundings, his sister, two years older than he, played a dominant role in his interpersonal relationships and in his struggles with sexual issues. She is described as having been boyish and unmanageable. The boy is reported to have felt very much oppressed by her merciless displays of superiority. It was the sister who initiated him into the sexual activity that was followed by his intense concerns about issues of sex difference. It was she who tricked him into getting into trouble by exhibiting his penis to his Nanya. She also played a significant part in the wolf phobia. It was she who delighted in arranging things so that he would be obliged to see the wolf picture and be reduced to helpless terror. In puberty when she rejected a sexual advance from him he sought out a servant girl of the same name and in sexual relations with her imagined the humiliation of his sister. The differentiation paradigm would draw attention to the possibility that a domineering older sister whose pleasure was to humiliate the boy and reduce him to helplessness might make it particularly difficult for a boy to resolve phase appropriate anxieties whose focus was feelings of envy of females, inferiority to them, and a sense that they caused his sense of lack.

Continuing, intensely conflicted feelings toward women permeate the case presentation. In the period before, during, and to some extent after the phobia the patient showed intense urges toward cruelty. Their focus was not males but females and their possessions, particularly his Nanya whom he not infrequently drove to tears, and small animals that represented babies to him. Toward the end of the phobic period he turned against women, though, significantly, not away from them. They, rather than males, remained focal in his interpersonal orientations. He asserted that he would never marry. He wondered why Adam in the biblical story had let himself be seduced by a woman. He thought of his sister as an evil spirit to be exorcised. When he emerged from confession he felt pure and good, but sensed always that his sister was there to tempt him to sin. In adulthood, too he had difficulties that suggest continued severe unresolved ambivalences toward women. He was able to fall in love only with women of the lower class and his love life was permeated by aims to debase women. He repeatedly announced that he could not bear to have to do with women, but was constantly and compulsively involved with them.

The available details of his relations to his mother and sister in adulthood suggest that one theme in his conflicts with women was sex-difference related feelings of envy of women and wishes to get back from them what he felt was rightly his. In his interactions with his mother and sister, Freud reports, the patient made furious and unwarranted attacks on them in relation to money matters. At one time when the father gave his sister two large bank notes the patient so furiously and vehemently attacked her and demanded a share of the money that she threw him all of it. When he heard the news of her death he consoled himself with the thought that now he would not have to share his parents' inheritance with her. After his father's death his mother administered the estate. Although the patient admitted that she was irreproachably liberal in meeting his financial demands he repeatedly created scenes in which he violently reproached her, accusing her of not loving him, of trying to economize at his expense, and of wishing he were dead so that she could have all the money for herself.

Freud suggests convincingly that the patient's associations made clear that in these scenes with his mother and sister the money represented babies. In the incident with the bank notes, he suggests, the patient was furious because he understood his sister to have gotten babies (sexual satisfaction) from the father. Similarly to have all the inheritance from his father for himself meant to him to have all his father's love, perceived in terms of sexual intercourse. Significantly, however, the patient's fury is reported as having been directed entirely at the sister, not the father who might have been held responsible for his deprivation. (Freud's interpretation of the patient's furious and unwarranted arguments with his mother about money matters takes a different turn. His sense was that they represented the patient's jealousy of her for having loved another child (his older sister) and possibly having wanted another child who would replace him, a theme that does not figure in his interpretation of the case as a whole.)

The differentiation model would invite clinical exploration of the possibility that a significant theme in the patient's rage at his mother and sister was related to the issue of babies in another way, specifically that babies (money) represented the femaleness women have and men do not. His envious and spiteful rage might be found to be focally directed toward the women, not only secondarily in relation to the father who gave babies to them rather than to him. Such a perspective would invite exploration of the patient's rage at the sister's possession of the two bank notes in terms of his feelings that she (the woman) got everything, he nothing. His satisfied reflection on hearing of her death, that now the total inheritance would be his might mean the converse to him, that now she had nothing and he everything. His quarrels with his mother too might be explored for similar meanings. The patient's accusations toward her were entirely unwarranted as they referred to financial matters. However, their character suggests the content of unresolved sex difference issues: She kept what was rightly his. She cheated him. She deprived him. She wanted everything for herself. She wished him dead so that she might have it all. In his accusations and demands one might see as well, his own covetous wishes to take what the mother (the female) has, to cheat her, to make her nothing (dead) so that he could have everything.

The Capacity to Give Birth as a Sex Difference Issue for Boys

The patient's questions about the origin of children permeate the case material. The importance of this issue for him is suggested by his intense positive and negative feelings toward babies and his focus on them as objects of both phobia and sadism. Freud reports the question of the origin of babies as one of the two major concerns that informed the boy's sexual researches prior to the dream and phobia. (The other was the possibility of not having a penis.) He describes a screen memory reported by the patient to the effect he had had a fit of rage because he had gotten too few presents for Christmas and that this had to do with an equation of presents with babies. In the stories of Little Red Riding Hood and The Wolf and the Seven Little Goats it was the thought of live children in the male wolf's belly that had intrigued him. He retained a memory of his Nanya's saying that he was his father's child and his sister the child of his mother and that this meant that he was born to his father. The wolf who has children inside occurs in associations to the dream that heralded the phobia and as the central phobic object. Among the phobias that accompanied this central one was a phobia of small animals who represented babies to him. Sadistic tormenting of small animals accompanied the phobias. In the subsequent obsessional neurosis the question of the origin of children reemerged in relation to the birth of Christ. And in adulthood the conflicts with his sister and mother, ostensibly about money, had additional meanings in his unconscious equation of money and babies.

In Freud's analysis of the case material, however, the patient's questions about the origin of babies play only a limited part with little or no relevance to issues of sex difference. Freud's interpretations are two-fold. First, babies had negative connotations for the boy as possible rivals for his mother's love, and second, they had positive meanings for him as they represented his willingness to give the father a baby in copulation with him. Differentiation theory would suggest, first, that the boy's positive feelings about babies did not concern only a willingness to give the father a baby in copulation with him, but concerned strong wishes to have the capacity to bear children, a capacity considered valuable in itself. Second, his concerns about having this capacity were not focused primarily on the father but on the mother. Third, a major focus of that concern was the question of a male being able to bear children as a female does. His negative feelings about babies seem not to be centered primarily on the possibility of the mother providing him with an unwanted rival for her love, but on her child-bearing capacities that he envies. Finally, evidence that these concerns permeated the anxiety dream and phobia, the subsequent obsessional neurosis, and later difficulties with women suggests that they were not peripheral for him, but a major source of conflict.

First, in the boy's positive feelings about babies there are significant themes that suggest that the capacity to bear children is a valued one in its own right (is not only a willingness accompanying his central wish to be copulated with by the father). The patient's remembered thought about the wolf in the two fairy tales, that maybe males could give birth suggests that he wished it were so. The stories themselves were important to him and linked by his interest in the babies being taken live from the wolf's body. In the dream that heralded the phobia the wolves are presents on the Christmas tree and Freud notes an associated screen memory of the boy being furious because he did not get the double lot of presents due him because his birthday fell on Christmas Day (and was thus a celebration of two births, his own, and that of Christ), and that in this memory presents represented babies. The boy's cruelty toward small animals who represented babies to him reflects not only dislike or hatred but also fascination.

Second, themes of bearing children appear to occur predominantly in relation to maternal figures (rather than, or not only, male ones), and in relation to them the issue appears to be one of one's own capacity to give birth (rather than, or not only, of the birth of a rival for the mother's love). The boy's curiosity about the wolf in the fairy tales was about his capacity to give birth as females could (not centrally as females could give babies to the male). In the obsessional neurosis his ruminations appear to concern questions as to who has the capacity to give birth to Christ (Mary, Joseph, or God) and who only *seems* to have that capacity (Joseph was only *like* a father; Mary was Christ's mother but God the true progenitor; God was Christ's father but Mary was the mother of God).

Third, a significant thread through the patient's associations and memories concerns the possibility of a male also being able to bear children (not only himself in a female role giving his father a child). In his question about the wolf in the fairy tales, as to whether perhaps a male too can bear children the issue is presented clearly and in the context of a knowledge of sex difference. His fantasy, retained well into middle childhood, that he was born of his father reiterates the notion that males can give birth. The obsessional ruminations about who gave birth to Christ seem again to suggest that it might have been a male or a female, and present the issue as a competitive one between males and females (Mary was Christ's mother, but God was his true progenitor; Mary, however, was the mother of God).

Finally, the evidence suggests that issues of child-bearing were not peripheral in the boy's concerns but were a significant focus of sex difference related conflict. A major contributor to the choice of the phobic object was the male wolf who, the boy wondered, might be able to give birth. The anxiety dream that preceded the phobia is permeated with imagery concerning the possibilities of a male having child-bearing capacities. The boy's sadistic mutilation and killing of small animals (babies) reflects not only hatred (or dislike of the idea of a possible rival) but a conflict in which fascination and hatred are combined. The concurrent phobias of small animals suggest elaborations of his intense but hostile involvement and concomitant fears of retribution. Issues of whether males or only females could give birth were important in the reported phenomena of his later obsessional neurosis and appear to have contributed to the violence of his later conflicts with his mother and sister about money.

Sex Difference and Anal Concerns

This patient had severe and longstanding anal difficulties and was intensely involved emotionally with the functioning of his bowels. For months at a time, in adulthood, he passed no stools unaided, but relied entirely on enemas given by an attendant. In childhood, bowel difficulties were evident in tendencies toward incontinence, constipation, and diarrhea. His identification of feces with money was suggested by his loss of bowel control in young adulthood on two occasions when the spending of money was at issue. His relationship with women seemed also to be expressed in anal terms. In the summer before the dream and phobia he defecated in his bed nightly while he shared a room with the English governess whom he hated. When at about age four and a half he defecated in his pants he expressed his shame and dismay in the words of his mother when she was complaining of her "female" abdominal difficulties. In his later sexual relations with women his interest focused strongly on their buttocks and on their have large broad hips, and he was most able to enjoy sexual intercourse if he entered the woman from behind. In his analysis with Freud anal issues made an early and striking appearance. Jones (1955) reports that in the patient's first meeting with Freud he offered to have rectal intercourse with him and to shit on his head.

In his analysis of these intestinal disorders Freud draws together two issues, the patient's wish to be copulated with by the father and his wish to bear children. He emphasizes the first and views the second as the patient's subsidiary willingness to give the father a baby in the context of his homosexual wish for sexual intercourse with him. Freud suggests that, following the castration threat from his Nanya, the boy gave up masturbation and a regression occurred from the genital to the anal instinctual organization. In this developmentally early context the boy retained notions that babies are excreted like feces and that the anus is the opening by which the man enters the woman sexually. The boy's cruelty to his Nanya and to small animals were expressions of his anal sadism. Provocative attempts to make his father punish him were masochistic reversals of the sadistic impulses. The obsessional neurosis that followed the phobic period was grounded in the boy's anal sadism. Its aim was the repression of the boy's wishes that the father have anal intercourse with him and his willingness in that context to give the father an (anal) baby. Such wishes made their disguised appearance in thought, about whether Christ had a behind and bowel movements, ruminations about who gave birth to Christ, continued beliefs that he was born of his father, and so forth. During this period fantasies about being beaten represented masochistic reversals of his continuing sadistic torture of small animals. In adulthood his violent quarrels with his mother and sister about money were disguised wishes to receive money (feces, babies) from the father as they had done. Masochistic reversals of sadistic impulses were represented in his dependence on his valet for enemas and his wish to be penetrated sexually by Freud.

The differentiation paradigm suggests that the mother as well as the father typically plays significant roles in the boy's anal difficulties. The boy's earliest ideas about giving birth, modeled on the digestive processes, do not take into account issues of sex difference. When these issues do become prominent, it is hypothesized, anally focused conflict may occur between the wish to retain the notion of the capacity to give birth and the recognition that males cannot do so. Feelings of envy and spite toward the mother who has what one does not may become intensified when, in the context of training in bowel control, she may seem to be depriving the boy of his body products or to be defining these valued possessions as waste material.

Such a model would invite clinical focus on the role of the mother in this patient's anal preoccupations. It would suggest that a major focus of his anal erotism was the wish to give birth, a capacity he conceived of in anal terms. It would offer, as well, a dynamic (rather than purely instinctual) hypothesis for the boy's sadism and suggest a possible additional theme in the masochistic reversal of his sadism.

The boy's initially unconflicted wish to be able to bear children is suggested in Freud's observation that the question of the origin of children was on one of two central questions that preoccupied the boy when he became interested in sexual matters in the period preceding the phobia. A beginning recognition that bearing children is sex specific is evident in his question about the wolf in the two fairy tales, as to whether he was female, because live babies were taken from his body, or whether males too could bear children. An equation of childbearing with anal activity and femaleness is vividly illustrated in his equation of his soiling problem with his mother's "female" difficulties.

In this context particular meanings of his anal sadism are suggested as well. The torturing of his beloved Nanya and small animals, to which Freud draws attention as an early expression of anal sadism, can be understood as combining ambivalent attraction toward with an envious wish to hurt females and their products (babies). A similar theme appears to occur in the anal sadism of the obsessional neurosis in which intrusive thoughts about "God-shit" or about Christ having a behind and shitting occurred in the context of ruminations about who could give birth. In adulthood the violent quarrels with his mother and sister about money (and equating money, feces, and babies), appear to have represented his wish for babies as Freud suggests, but were also sadistic attacks on the women in which he accused them of getting everything and demanded that they give him what was rightly his. His relations with women generally in adulthood combined compulsive falling in love with violent repudiation in the context of strongly anal interests (in women's buttocks, in entering them from behind) and wishes to debase them. That is, a differentiation model would suggest that this boy's anal sadism was directed largely toward females and that it combined fascination with femaleness and the babies that are its product with repudiation and envious wishes to hurt and humiliate what is female.

Freud draws attention to the masochistic reversal of the boy's sadistic wish to torment in provocative attempts to make his father punish him, and, in the obsessional period, in fantasies of being beaten (apparently by males). He suggests that in adulthood the patient's dependence on his valet for enemas and his wish that Freud penetrate him sexually, represented masochistic reversals of sadistic impulses but he does not specify the primary sadistic impulses of which these were the reversals. A differentiation paradigm would suggest that the patient's masochism was, in part, a reversal of his sadistic wishes to hurt what is female. The possible reversal is most evident in his adult relations with women and the relation to his valet and Freud. In the masochistic reversal of his sadistic wish to take from women and hurt them it is the male (the valet, Freud) who enters *him* from behind and (as in an enema, and perhaps in an analysis) takes forcibly from him what he will not relinquish voluntarily.

The Place of the Father

The boy's view of father as a powerful, dominant male is central in Freud's formulation of the major themes in this case. His conflict is seen to be between his biologically based masculinity and his femininity, the former expressed in competitive rivalry with the father and fear of retaliative castration from him, the latter in a wish to be copulated with by him. In his elaboration of this formulation, however, two groups of observations troubled Freud. First, the patient seemed not to perceive males as powerful but as weak and castrated. His predominant images of males were of servants, beggars and cripples, of his father as weak and ill, and of a mute day laborer of whom he had been fond. Second, the patient's castration imagery referred to women rather than men. Freud recognized that these observations posed problems for his conceptualization but he was unable to find a satisfactory resolution of them.

The differentiation framework proposes a different place for the father in this boy's gender development. It suggests that in the period before the recognition of sex difference this father was available to the patient, but that in consequence of illness he was not able to play his appropriate roles when the boy became aware of sex difference and in the later competitive rivalry of the oedipus complex. The illness is by no means fully described in the case presentation but Freud does report that the boy's father suffered repeated attacks of severe depression, and that when, at age six; the boy visited him in a sanatarium he had been away from home for "many months."

As far as can be ascertained, this patient's gender development was within normal limits in the first of these three phases. He had developed a basic sense of himself as masculine (rather than, for example, as a female in a male body, as in the transsexual men Stoller describes (1968)). He appears to have identified with his father in wishes to grow up to be like him. In the dream and phobia, as Freud points out, his basic commitment to masculinity is consistently evident, and it is central to his conflicts between wishes he is reluctant to give up which are, however, incompatible with his being male.

Developmental issues of the third phase, that centrally involving oedipal issues, are not evident in more than rudimentary form. The hallmark of that phase is the boy's sense of himself as male in rivalry with his father perceived as a powerful male, wishing to take his place (centrally with the mother), and fearing annihilating defeat (castration).

The dream and phobia show little evidence of such struggles with the father. In the stories which figured prominently in his memory, (Little Red Riding Hood and The Wolf and Seven Little Goats), the wolf is not in competition with another male. His focus on the female is not a wish to make her his own to the exclusion of other males. His annihilation occurs not in competitive defeat by the male but in punishment for his attempt to usurp what belongs to the female. (Associations to the dream, though not the phobia, also deal with a story in which the tailor pulls the tail off a wolf. In these associations a male damages another male, and, although there is little evidence in the story or in the associations, of male competition for a female or for other goals, the occurrence of these associations may reflect the presence of oedipal issues in at least elementary form.)

Similarly, the evidences of masculinity that Freud reports as occurring prior and subsequent to the dream do not suggest masculine rivalry with another male. The boy's concerns about the possibility that a person might not have a penis do not yet occur, as might be the case in the later developmental stage, in the context of a triadic relationship in which the boy perceives himself to be in a same-sex relationship to the father, and both himself and his father in cross-sex relations to the mother. In the subsequent obsessional neurosis the male relationship symbolized in the relation of Christ and God shows little evidence of oedipal rivalry or competition. The reported observations of the patient's difficulties with adult sexuality do not have the stamp of male competition, wishes to usurp another man's place with a woman, or fear of retaliation by another man (originally the father) for intimacy with a woman. Finally, though the reported material concerning his adulthood is very limited, there is little indication of competitive or affiliative relations with men—a sense of himself as a man among men—in his social or occupational life.

Issues of the second phase, that in which sex difference is the major focus, do seem central in the patient's experience. His focus on the female as having what he does not has been elaborated. The two groups of observations Freud could not integrate with his conceptualization find a ready place: When issues of sex difference are central the boy tends to believe, though in normal development only transiently, that to be male is to be in some central way to be lacking, and during that period too, it is the mother rather than the father who is seen as the depriver (castrator).

The father's role in this phase is hypothesized to be important in particular ways. The father may be a source of reassurance to the boy that to be male does not mean to be lacking or damaged. He may offer the boy possibilities of identification and relationship which provide a bulwark against regressive urges to merge with the mother. And in relationship to him the boy may find refuge from being altogether embroiled in the feelings of deprivation, envy and spite which may threaten to overwhelm him in his feelings toward females.

There are suggestions in the clinical material that it was in these areas that the boy most sorely missed his father. In various ways he tried to establish bonds with males. After the early seduction by his sister that occurred in the father's absence, the boy, on the father's return, attempted in various ways to be punished by him. Freud interprets these as attempts at seduction (in which the boy would take a female role with the father), but they may also have been attempts to establish an alliance with the father in which the father would forcefully support the boy in the control of impulses before which he felt helpless. During his later boyhood the patient used his relation to his confessor to re-establish feelings of being pure and innocent, but feared always that beyond the confessional his sister lay in wait to tempt him to sin. At about age ten he was able to use a relationship with a male tutor to identify with masculine interests, and at his instigation to give up his sadistic torturing of small animals.

The boy's continuing painful sense of lack in his relationship to his father as helper appears to be represented, too, in his preoccupations about the relationship of Christ and God during the period of his obsessional neurosis. Freud interpreted these as reflections of the (positive) Oedipus complex. They seem, however, to have little to do with feelings toward the castrating father of oedipal rivalry, and instead to reflect the boy's feelings about a father who is unavailable in times of need. The patient's feelings about the cruelty of God, which he recalled in adulthood, had to do with God's unwillingness to identify his son as his own, his unresponsiveness to his son's pleas for help, his abandoning his son to those who wanted to hurt him, his allowing all sorts of wickedness and tormenting to go on when he could have made men good. When, shortly before Christ's crucifixion, the mob demanded a miracle to prove that Christ was his son, God made no miracle. When Christ prayed that if possible God take this cup (his approaching death) from him, God did not answer. The personal theme that appears to underly these preoccupations is the patient's sense of having been inexplicably abandoned by his father to the tormented and tormenting relationships he had with others, just at the time when he most needed reassurance from him.

SUMMARY

In the case of the Wolf Man Freud discusses a young boy's reactions to the recognition of sex difference. His focus is the boy's struggles to cope with female orientations that he recognizes to be incompatible with his ego-syntonic maleness. The theoretical framework for the discussion is primarily Freud's theory of bisexuality, of a constitutionally based masculinity and feminity that occurs in all individuals. From that perspective the boy's difficulties are seen as struggles between the actualization of his biologically based femininity (in wishes to take the female role in copulation with a male) and a recognition that to do so would mean giving up his maleness.

The differentiation model suggests an alternative theoretical framework for understanding boys' struggles with issues of femininity when they become aware of sex difference. The case material lends itself to a comparison of this perspective with Freud's in five areas. Notions of wished for bisexual completeness appear to be represented in the dream and phobia central to Freud's discussion and in subsequent disturbances as well. The mother (not only the father) appears to occupy a central place in the boy's conflicts, in feelings of envy, deprivation, and spite. The femaleness that preoccupies him seems to have to do with child-bearing capacities he now recognizes to be exclusively female and ruled out for him. His struggles about giving up these capacities appear to contribute significantly to the patient's long-standing anal problems. The place of the father in this period is perceived differently than in Freud's model. Rather than being viewed as the powerful male with whom the boy wishes to take a female role he is seen normally to offer the boy a model of undamaged maleness and a haven from the turmoil of his sex difference related conflicts with females. It appears that illness prevented this patient's father from taking this role and that the boy felt the lack keenly.

REFERENCES

Brunswick, R. M. (1928/1950). A supplement to Freud's "History of an Infantile Neurosis." In *The Psychoanalytic Reader,* ed. R. Fliess. London: Hogarth Press Ltd.

Freud, S. (1918). From the history of an infantile neurosis. *S.E.* 17, 7–123.

Jones, E. (1955). *The life and works of Sigmund Freud, Vol. II.* New York: Basic Books.

Stoller, R. J. (1968). *Sex and Gender, Vol. 1.* New York: Jason Aronson.

Index